IRELAND IN 2050

HOW WE WILL BE LIVING

STEPHEN KINSELLA

CONTENTS

ACKNOWLEDGEMENTS

This book started life as an eight-hundred-word rant in the *Irish Times*, which ran on 6 August 2008. Thanks to Willy Clingan for running with the piece, and to the readers of the *Irish Times* for making that article the most popular on *www.irishtimes.com* for more than a week.

Thanks to Peter and Seán from Liberties Press for approaching me to expand that little rant into the much larger one you are holding in your hands.

Thanks for the support of the extremely professional staff at Liberties Press – Daniel Bolger, Orlaith Delaney and Caroline Lambe. Thomas Morris provided excellent research assistance.

Special thanks go to my very good friend Nick Young, who read successive early drafts. His comments improved the book considerably. Gerard O'Neill kindly read portions of an early draft, and gave comments that changed the direction of two of the chapters. Jim and Dagmar gave me somewhere to hide to write. My parents, Gay and Mary, and my brothers, Peter and Mick, put up with my ranting on a daily basis. Pity them, dear reader.

To my colleagues in the Kemmy Business School at the University of Limerick, thanks for many stimulating conversations on the various subject areas of this book. My mentor and friend Prof. K. Vela Velupillai deserves special thanks for making me the economist I am today – obsessed with telling useful stories about the real world. The duty of a mentor is to provide expert training and unflagging encouragement. I have received both in spades.

Without the support of my wife, Elke, I wouldn't have finished college, let alone a book. You make my life better every day.

I wrote this book for my second son Cillian, whose existence, along with his brother Arran, got me thinking about the Ireland I'd like them to live in, and the one they might end up with, if we're not careful.

Prologue: One Fine Day

1 January 2050

Less than fifteen thousand days away from today

Jack Murphy is not a happy camper. His car won't start. The year is 2050 and the bloody car won't start! His partner Sarah echoes his frustration, and reminds him just how late they are going to be, and reminds him that she reminded him to charge the car last night. Which he obviously didn't. Jack says nothing to this. Herding twelve-year-old Bobby into the back seat and strapping him in, Jack finally charges the car to 30 per-cent of the full battery power and removes the plug from the wall of his house. The car starts with a whirr and trundles down the driveway towards the main road. This car is knackered, he thinks. Time to print a new one.

Traffic is light, and Jack makes fairly good time as the car descends from the Dublin mountains. Reports of local flooding seem to have been exaggerated. That, or the local authority's environmental clean-up crew is very efficient today.

Sarah wishes Jack a happy birthday. Jack is forty-one years old today, born on New Year's Day 2009, and doesn't really want to think about birthdays. A broadcast tells him that the National Asset Management Agency, created in 2009 to clean up the effects of a property crash, has just been formally wound up. Talk about economics irritates Jack, so he switches the broadcast off.

Because Jack forgot to charge the car, Jack and Sarah's daughter, Maeve, is late for her prenatal class at the local health care clinic – and not happy about it. Maeve is seventeen years old, and this is her first combined consultation and lesson.

Sarah, a nurse, thinks Maeve is probably five or six weeks along. Maeve is waiting to find out the sex of the baby at the birth, and talk of how to decorate the baby's room (yellows? greens? blues?) fills the car until they reach their destination. Nobody can decide on what to eat tonight, so they drop the subject. Nobody mentions the fact that Maeve's boyfriend, Patrick, hasn't called in a week.

Maeve gets out with just a little difficulty, and waves goodbye. She's caught in a cloud of dust as Jack speeds off to drop Bobby to secondary school. He then drops Sarah in to work, before finally making it to the office himself. Jack feels tired by the time he gets into his company's newly leased office space, but doesn't let it show as he shuffles through the door and greets his co-workers, apologising for being late.

Jack's co-workers knew that he was running late, because they have the GPS signal of Jack's phone and car. They asked the car for an ETA, and rescheduled the meeting Jack was supposed to chair accordingly. Draping his coat over the back of his office chair, Jack reaches for a cup of coffee and downs it in one, glad he insisted on the expensive stuff when his company bought a coffee maker. This coffee is twenty-five euro a cup, but it's worth every drop. Best bit about it is, the coffee's Irish.

Jack is the co-director, chief creative consultant, chief technology officer, and head bottle-washer of a small firm specialising in three-dimensional embeddings of advertising into online media.

Jack's company want the logos on the screens people see all around them to be clickable. They want to get paid for developing and rolling out this new technology, as well as getting paid on a per-click basis by the firms that license the technology.

Jack's company directly employs four people: three in Ireland and one in Bangalore, India, but Jack outsources many of the firm's more mundane functions to non-contract virtual labour, or online virtual assistants. All told, Jack's company has worked with more than a thousand different providers in its short existence, all of them selling niche services, like fabrication, coding, human resources, taxation and legal services, to Jack's company.

Jack and his co-workers will be filthy rich soon – once their technology is mature enough to be bought up by one of the large corporations at whom the business is targeted. They hope.

Jack's idea can't fail.

His previous thirteen have, though.

This is Jack's fourteenth company start-up in twelve years. He and two college friends had been mildly successful with one business venture – their first, which took off. When they sold the start-up to a large corporation, Jack's family became financially secure at a more or less middle-class level. Clever asset management of the returns from his first business, along with some funding from venture capitalists and a trickle from government grants, keeps Jack afloat today.

This idea just can't fail. The rest of the group's ideas have simply not worked out: for each subsequent start-up, their ideas were either ahead of their time, slightly behind the market, or just plain wrong. Each time the company folded, the partners retreated to lick their wounds; a month or two later, they started a new project, with a new idea.

Jack scans his messages, sees one from Maeve, but doesn't read it. Jack and his team have a brief meeting, decide what to do next. Then the four-person company gets to work for the day. An alert from Bobby's school comes through. Jack reads it and grimaces. Then he laughs.

At the moment, Jack and his colleagues are worried about the rising price of doing business in China. China's economy has fragmented, with power having shifted from the once-monolithic Communist Party to competing regional assemblies. These assemblies impose differing rules for foreign investors like Jack, and complying with these overlapping rules and regulations is starting to get expensive.

Many of the more mundane coding and packaging jobs the firm needs are done in China, and with the Chinese economy still growing, albeit in fits and starts, the added pressure of exchange-rate fluctuations, and higher wage demands on his business, has Jack thinking about terminating his relationship with his Chinese subcontractors and returning to his US contacts. But Jack can't conclude one set of business relationships until he can find another company, or set of companies, which is equally as good. This is no mean feat; and while he searches, his costs are going up. Jack is getting worried, because his margins are tight, and he doesn't want to have to sell more equity in the firm or dip into his nest egg. He runs his hands through his thinning hair. Just then, he gets a call about dinner from Sarah.

Sarah Hayes is forty-three years old, born in 2007 to proud parents in Leitrim. She looks thirty-one, and she knows it – which makes her happy. Her job as a nurse in Dublin keeps her on her toes, while two children at home make sure she doesn't have time to waste. Sarah is busy every day because the demand for medical staff on an hourly basis in her hospital is very high – though that demand fluctuates wildly. Sarah works in one of Ireland's public hospitals, so she sees the sickest, and the poorest, in Irish society. Those with relatively mild complaints are seen in a local clinic, like the one Sarah's daughter Maeve went to earlier that morning. The better-off in Irish society take their illnesses to private hospitals, while the relatively poor must queue. And queue. And queue.

The system Sarah works in is well-managed and efficient, if continually strained, and her colleagues are well-trained, though morale could be higher. Talk of pay cuts is on everyone's lips, and has been for years now. Supplies of drugs are not an issue here, at least for the moment. International agreements on bulk drug purchases by nations within the EU continue to hold, and the drugs continue to flow into the hospitals. For now.

Ireland's relationship with the EU is in jeopardy, and hospital administrators are trying to plan what to do if the EU-wide bulk drug purchase scheme goes south, increasing the price of drugs and further curtailing the service Sarah and her colleagues can provide to the poorest in Ireland.

After getting out of the car and saying goodbye hurriedly, Sarah walks into the Accident and Emergency department of her hospital, and scans a comprehensive set of online decision-management tools fed by a patient's test results and their previous medical records, placed at Sarah's disposal to help with diagnoses and treatment plans, and to speed up patient throughput. 'Treat, then street' is the rule. But in reality the rule isn't followed to the letter, because reality doesn't show up on diagnostic screens very often.

There are only a few doctors, nurses, technicians and other health care professionals relative to the numbers of people coming into the emergency room every day, so queues and delays are inevitable.

Ireland's faltering universal health care system, combined with a large older population, means that Sarah is kept busy all day. She likes this because it makes her shift go faster.

Sarah gets a message from Maeve, but doesn't have time to open it. She doesn't open the message from Bobby's school, either. Some days she just can't wait to get off work, but in general the casework is interesting and the people are nice, and so, most of the time, Sarah gets through her shift in good form. Every night as she leaves, she makes a note of the face of the last person in the door of the emergency room. If she sees the same person in the emergency room the next morning, she knows it's going to be a bad day.

Sarah's father, Jim, gives her a call: does she want him to cook dinner for them all that night?

Jim Hayes is a recently retired local politician. At seventy-two, he's in good shape, thanks to lifelong addictions to golf and tennis, but he's been feeling weaker lately. Jim was elected to local office in 2009 for the first time, at the age of forty-one, and is currently writing his political memoirs, called *The Face of 1978* – a reference to his birth year. Jim also works on small community projects in the Dublin area, and has recently completed a nature-walk rezoning, redevelopment and redesign near Jack's house.

Sarah's phone has access to Jim's recent medical records, and she makes the phone take Jim's pulse as he talks to her. He seems fine now, but Sarah is a little worried. She says none of this to Jim, but makes a note to talk to Jack about arranging a physical for his father in the near future, and consider looking at community care options.

Jim dotes on his two grandchildren. He knows he is lucky to have two of them. Kids are few and far between these days.

Sarah, feeling overworked and remembering the family's indecision about dinner in the car that morning, is happy to accept Jim's offer. She puts in a call to Maeve and Bobby and lets them know that Granddad will be cooking dinner.

Jim's phone asks Sarah's fridge what they have in the house, and places an order for steaks, before hanging up. The fridge tells Jim it got them a good deal on steaks. Jim isn't so sure. He's never really trusted the decisions of fridges.

Then Jim gets back to work.

Jim is writing a chapter on local authorities in Ireland, and the battles he fought as a younger man in 2015 and 2016 to reform those small, powerless entities into larger, more autonomous organisations with real political clout, but with a smaller footprint in the Irish political system.

Jim is trying to figure out just why he lost those battles, and why only a public outcry forced their partial reform. Planning disruptions caused by compulsory purchase orders and local authority inefficiencies meant that levees designed to stop flooding in Dublin's docklands and Limerick city took five years longer than necessary.

The flooding cost the government billions, and began a steady increase in the national debt – which the current administration is starting to pay down, thanks to the tax windfall they have received through a boom in demand for Irish products and workers from a resurgent US economy.

Just as he is starting to feel upset for the umpteenth time about his failure to put these thoughts down coherently, Jim receives a message from Maeve which makes him smile.

Twelve-year-old Bobby hates school. He is not naturally bookish, but he doesn't like sport and has few friends. He also has a large amount of group-work to do for his various classes. His parents worry that he might be getting bullied.

Bobby's first year in secondary school is not going well. Faced with the prospect of five more years of this crap, Bobby turns to his computer and begins recording haikus about steaks made from teachers. Bobby's teacher's monitoring program spots Bobby's transgression from the designated class feed and gives Bobby one demerit, meaning that he'll do detention this time.

Bobby is not impressed, but his mood quickly lightens, as his group wins a prize for their recent data visualisation project. The group's idea was to model word usage in Irish to try and sense patterns in the evolution of the language over the forty-eight years since the creation of TnaG, the Irish 'television' station, though Bobby doesn't know anybody who watches a 'television' except his grandfather.

Bobby's group finds little change in the Irish language relative to the English language over the same period, but their estimation method was novel, and so the group was awarded first prize. Bobby still has to do his detention. He returns to being unimpressed and thinks of India.

His father's businesses meant that Bobby and Maeve travelled with them quite a bit, especially when they were younger.

Sarah took a leave of absence from her job at the hospital, and the family settled for a year in Bangalore, India. Sarah didn't like it there, but the prospects looked good for Jack's business, at least for a while. Bobby and Maeve loved it in India. Everything seemed so modern, relative to Ireland. Bobby still feels a bit dislocated by the move back to Ireland. He just can't settle.

Bobby's next class involves comparative religion. His group is creating a mash-up of different faith-based songs on the theme of redemption. Bobby's group have picked betrayal, and he is surprised to find Gregorian chanting so appealing, but is uninterested in the project generally. Bobby's teacher warns him about daydreaming again, and Bobby's bad mood returns. He remembers that he still has to do detention. Bah.

Maeve is not waiting long to see her gynaecologist. Her mother Sarah's private health insurance more than covers the cost of prenatal care, and so Maeve is seen quickly. The examination reveals nothing out of the ordinary with the baby, and Maeve saves a movie of her child's face to her phone, sending it to Jim, Sarah, Jack and a few of her friends. Maeve discusses birthing options with her midwife, and opts for a home birth, which is standard. There's not much to worry about, as Maeve knows that Sarah will be at hand to help with the birth. She is worried about what Jack will say. She knows that Jack is not too happy with the pregnancy, and Maeve is sure that her grandfather disapproves of her having a child at such a young age. She thinks that they think that her education and career will suffer. Maeve thinks that her father and her grandfather are both wrong. Maeve messages her boyfriend Patrick, but gets no answer.

Maeve's prenatal class starts directly after her exam. The expectant mothers are taught basic parenting skills like time management, how to do developmental checks on their babies, and basic hygiene, as well as learning coping mechanisms, work strategies and other tips and tricks. They will need all of these tools to cope with raising a child in the mid-twenty-first century. Maeve and her classmates are given readings to study on their phones, and parenting resource feeds are added for her by her instructor to look at later.

Maeve's mind drifts, and she becomes excited at the thought of running her own business, like her father; she then becomes discouraged when she thinks of how the businesses her dad sets up don't work out. She thinks she might opt for a career in law, or even medicine. There's still so much time, she tells herself.

And she's right.

Maeve will probably live to be ninety-five, so she thinks that a few years given over to child-rearing isn't really a waste of anything. Maeve does the sums. She will live to be ninety-five. She wants at most two children, so that's eighteen months or so spent just being pregnant – less than 2 percent of her life. If she has the children three years apart, and the children enter the school system at five years of age, she can get back to work outside the home when the oldest (she hopes she has a boy first, then a girl) begins school.

Total time spent exclusively minding children: eight years – less than 8 percent of her life. Best to get the child-rearing over early, she feels. But Maeve is also a little scared. Maeve begins to worry about the baby's future – born in 2050 in Dublin and facing into an uncertain future. Then she tells herself that all new parents think this way, and goes back to studying the documents she was given at the parenting course. A message comes through to Maeve from the fridge. Because she is the closest, she will have to go and pick up the steaks for the dinner tonight. They're ready: the fridge has told her so.

The class is nearly over. Maeve gets ready to leave, and gets up, just a little slowly. She's getting the bus home, and isn't looking forward to it.

1

Writing a History of Ireland's Future

The power of an imagined end, and it literally can only be imagined, lies in its ability to influence present choices.

DANIEL TAYLOR[1]

Why we should put ourselves out of our way to do anything for posterity, for what has posterity ever done for us?

SIR BOYLE ROCHE[2]

We are suffering just now from a bad attack of economic pessimism[3]. The Irish economy is in free fall, its once-spectacular economic growth dragged down to depression levels by the twin weights of a property crash and an international economy in financial turmoil. Unemployment is once again the national obsession. The prospect of mass emigration has returned for the first time in a generation. Uncertainty abounds.

There is an emerging view that the good times are over for the foreseeable future, that belts must be tightened, costs contained, people let go, expectations reduced. Ireland's workers must once again leave our shores in search of the rewarding work – and the attendant prosperity – they fleetingly enjoyed here. The man on the street believes with some certainty that a decline in Irish prosperity is more likely than an improvement in the decade that lies ahead of us to 2020[4].

I believe the man in the street is wrong. I believe we are suffering from the growing pains of extremely rapid structural changes in the international economy and at home, as well as the economic hangover any burst bubble generates. I believe our economy has developed faster than our mindsets, and I believe the prevailing international recession (and perhaps, depression) and our fragile domestic situation, though both are very serious, blind us to the changes that have taken place under the surface of Ireland's economy and society. Despite our current troubles, I believe Ireland is in forward motion, and I want to use this book to show you where we came from, where we are, and convince you of my beliefs as to where we're headed as a country. This book is an effort to explain the possibilities our grandchildren might face by 2050, and to place our current situation, dire as it is, in some perspective. I'd like to reintroduce a sense of proportion to our thinking – something that I believe we've lost in recent years.

As bad as today's economic woes are relative to the boom times we were experiencing just a year or two ago, they are just part of an episode in Irish economic history. The Irish economy will recover. This depression too shall pass.

And where will we be then?

The book you're holding attempts to answer this question.

I predict with some certainty that, depending on your position in life right now – your age, your health, your family's health, whether you've a job or not – that position will colour how you are going to read this book. So it is with everyone. I hope that I can show you overly pessimistic outlooks of a grim, smog-filled future that only violent societal change can remedy are misplaced – although as a nation we certainly face serious threats to our nation from climate change, inequality, energy security, and our ageing population.

I want to convince you that the balance of our social and economic lives is just not that fragile. The Irish people can accommodate changes of breathtaking scale and scope to their daily lives, and those of their children and grandchildren. I know this because we have weathered worse in the history of our nation.

We are now as far away from 1970 as we are from 2050.

You might think that everything will change in the next forty years, but you'd be wrong. Think about the main street where you live. I'll bet it hasn't changed all that much from the street you remember as a child. A few new shops, new coats of paint, perhaps a new road surface, but ultimately, all the same. Somewhere to buy milk; something to drive on to get to the shop to buy the milk. The details might change, but the dynamic remains the same.

Take a look at the pictures of Dublin's O'Connell Street, on the next page. They are strikingly similar. We see the same buildings, and the same streets. The buses and a few monuments are different, but it remains, fundamentally, the same from 1970 to 2009. Satellite images of Dublin over the same period show a huge increase outward into neighbouring counties.

Over a stretch of forty years, Ireland experienced change

26

only incrementally, in discrete lumps, and at different speeds. The time scale isn't really long enough to notice fundamental shifts in the character of the nation, although of course we can point to areas where things have changed a lot – the public attitude to the Catholic Church, the level of home ownership, regional and industrial development, and so on.

Ireland's development over the last forty years, though striking (both in how we failed to develop from 1970 – 1987, and how quickly we developed thereafter), hasn't changed us all that much. The influence of the Catholic Church is much diminished. We drink more cappuccinos, and owe more money per person, and we travel more. But fundamentally, today we are the same. We'll be fundamentally the same in forty years.

Things just haven't changed that much.

Figure 1: O'Connell Street in 1970. Notice the buses, the buildings, and the monuments, all similar to today. Source: *www.teachnet.ie*

Figure 2: O'Connell Street in 2009. Source: *www.wikiimages.com*

WHY BOTHER WRITING A HISTORY OF THE FUTURE?

Writing the history of the future is much harder than writing the history of the past. Difficulties arise when futurologists simply extrapolate trends. Forecasting is a bit like trying to drive a car by looking out the back windows only. For example, we see that right now the world's population is going up, so if it keeps going up at the same rate, in 2050 we'll have 20 billion people or something – that sort of calculation is too error-prone to be really useful outside of a short time horizon. In 1968, Fiat CEO Aurelio Peccei founded the Club of Rome. He wanted to find solutions to the 'global problematique' – the series of ever-deepening and converging crises he saw happening in the developed world in the late twentieth century. He hired a group of scientists to model and predict the course of industrial society; this group produced the 1972 best-seller, *The Limits to Growth*. This book told a simple truth: on a planet endowed with finite resources, not everyone can develop indefinitely forever. As populations grew and economic growth shuddered to a halt, the need to provide food, shelter, water, energy and other raw materials would split industrial societies in half, between the rich and the poor. The natural resources of the Earth – typically modelled as oil, gas and coal, as well as agricultural land – could only support so many individual usages, could only absorb so much pollution. When only a few of these resources became scarce and expensive, the processes they drove would unravel and upset the apple cart of industrial societies. Once the population in each country overshot what the researchers called 'the carrying capacity' of that country, the twin costs of resource depletion and environmental pollution rise faster than the rate of growth. The economic burden of dealing with these costs rapidly plunges the society into internal political chaos, war, or both.

The hypotheses presented in *The Limits to Growth* have been widely discussed, verified, falsified, and verified again. There were many reasons in the 1970s to believe the critics of modern economic growth: soaring oil prices and other energy costs, US military failure in Vietnam, Ireland's sluggish performance relative to our European neighbours. In Ireland, the fear was of a population explosion: between 1978 and 1980, more than 100,000 children were born – a figure only eclipsed in 2008 and 2009. Increasing birth rates were going to cause global and national catastrophes – but these forecasts have turned out to be inaccurate.

If history has taught us one thing, it is that Ireland's population can fluctuate wildly in a fairly short space of time, thanks to migration inwards and outwards, so we should approach talk of ever-growing populations with some scepticism.

Another example, which keeps getting trotted out in debates about the future of the 'European' model, and Ireland's place in that model, is productivity growth (the idea that somehow American workers in an hour of work do more than European workers, and have been doing so for some time). It is a well-established fact that US workers work more hours, and produce more stuff, than European workers.

There is a natural tendency amongst commentators to assume this productivity gap will persist forever, and get even wider as the years roll on. A crisis will develop, some say, and this crisis will force the EU to make drastic institutional changes, which will hurt everyone. Quick! Better to start

29

remaking the European Union along US and Anglo-Saxon lines now to avoid the inevitable pain. The argument I've given above, and those like it, are variants on the old saying 'a stitch in time saves nine'. That argument will crop up many times in these pages. Sometimes the argument is valid, other times its use is self-serving and potentially dangerous.

'GO BACK TO DRIVING A TRUCK'

Think how hard it is to predict a winner in any field. Take sport. Dublin played Kerry recently in GAA Football. Every pundit had the same opinion: Kerry as a football force were on the slide. Their recent form told of a team who were 'tired', 'rudderless' and due a drubbing by a resurgent Dublin side whose recent form was stellar. The bookies gave odds suggesting the match was Dublin's to lose. Yet the men from Kerry blasted Dublin off the pitch that day, leaving Dublin supporters (and the bookies) asking 'why us' this year.

In publishing, J. K. Rowling, author of the Harry Potter series of books, had her first book turned down several times. She has since become one of the richest people on Earth.

In music, predicting a winner is even harder. The Beatles, the band that defined a generation, were rejected by one EMI executive, as he thought 'guitar bands are out of fashion'. One Mr E. Presley was fired in 1954 from a touring gig and told 'you ain't going nowhere son. Go back to driving a truck'. In 1895, a young boy's father was told by the boy's teacher that 'it doesn't matter what he does, he will never amount to anything'. The boy did amount to something. His name was Albert Einstein[5].

In finance, picking a winner is very, very hard.

Professional analysts spend their lives trying to anticipate up or down ticks in the markets. Economists fare worse than anybody.

In 1929, Irving Fisher of Yale University, a respected professor and stock market analyst, reassured the public that 'Stocks have reached what looks like a permanently high plateau'[6]. Those same stocks were to fall precipitously over the next five years as the 'Great Depression' took hold and destroyed the wealth of a generation in the process. The Irish Stock Exchange was told by the Irish Banking Federation in June 2007 that its fundamentals were still strong, only to watch banks listed on the main Irish index of shares, the ISEQ, lose up to 98 percent of their value in eighteen months.

So: take a pinch of salt with you while reading this book, and every other book that deals with the future in this way. The real reason for thinking about the future at all, is to give ourselves a sense of story, that we can in some sense change our current behaviour to alter the story we might see playing out for ourselves.

Taking a longer view also gives you grounds to question current topics in a different context, and gives us the confidence to say 'this too shall pass'. Going back to the national productivity argument, in the 1980s it was all the rage to argue that Japan would beat the US in manufacturing, that the US needed to take on Japanese work practices and that, one day, Japan would end up owning the US. By the mid-1990s, Japan was an economic basket case, and has only recently recovered. For everyone currently talking about reforming Ireland's institutions along US (or Chinese) lines, taking a longer view will serve us well.

THIS TOO SHALL PASS – UNLESS IT DOESN'T

The next reason for talking about a longer stretch of time is that most of us are likely to live to see it, but we don't necessarily act as if we will: if you are thirty in 2009, you'll only be seventy-one in 2050. Research by the Irish Pensions Board[7] on pensions provision for women in their thirties in Ireland bears this point out nicely, and though the argument applies equally to men, because more men are in pensionable jobs, the need to equip women with pensions is more urgent. Only 50.6 percent of women in Ireland have pension coverage, compared to 58.3 percent of men. Given that in 2050 you might have twenty, thirty or even more years to run in your life, it is worth giving some thought now as to how you're going to live your life for your remaining years.

The table on the next page shows three important facts. First, the numbers in work are scheduled to stay roughly constant, at around 2 million workers. Second, those aged over sixty-five are expected to increase by more than 300 percent as our society ages. Third, the numbers of people at work supporting those who are over sixty-five will drop precipitously, from 4.3 to 1.4 people at work supporting one person who is retired. There is an urgent need to think about how to solve this problem, and as I write this, the public dialogue on coming up with solutions to this problem is virtually nonexistent.

One of the most important and beautiful features of human life is that actions we take today affect our futures, often in ways we can't predict. Our beliefs about tomorrow – our expectations, social scientists would say – change our actions today, and by acting differently today, we change the conditions we experience tomorrow.

	2006	2026	2056
Numbers at work	2,000,100	2,268,000	2,125,000
Aged over 65	464,000	844,000	1,532,000
Numbers at work per person over 65	4.3	2.7	1.4

Table 1. Ireland's workforce won't change, but our demography will. The numbers of young people supporting older people will decrease as our society ages. Source: Irish Pensions Board, *www.pensionsboard.ie.*

Confidence matters. Say the whole world makes, buys, and sells only cars. I have a feeling I'm going to be laid off soon. Will I go out and buy a new car? Not likely. If everyone thinks that way, then much fewer cars are bought, our little economy goes into a recession, and I get laid off. The third reason for writing a book about the distant future is that current conditions affect expectations about the future, which changes present behaviour, and changes the future. By writing a story about an imagined future, as the quote from Daniel Taylor at the start of this chapter shows, we can think coherently about changes we might make today to forestall or encourage parts of that imagined future.

It is highly dangerous for us not to have this conversation. Roche's quote above asking what posterity has done for the present is the opposite of Taylor's view. We have too many like Roche in our public conversation. We need more Daniel Taylors.

A lack of discussion about Ireland's future is dangerous, because without a long-term sense of direction, we constantly make short-term choices, and these may not be in the best interests of the nation. I'm not saying we need a five-year, Stalinist plan. I don't think these types of exercises are fruitful, because we don't have enough information about the present to plan in a meaningful way for the future at that level of detail. Rather, a set of national, regional, local and personal priorities could be arrived at – if we start talking about the future now. If present decisions were framed in terms of these national priorities, then we could adopt a coherent strategy toward whatever challenges we might face as a nation.

I don't have a crystal ball. In fact, I would be delighted if every word in this book turns out to be completely wrong – if the book begins a debate about the type of Ireland Irish people would like to see for their grandchildren and indeed for themselves as they get older.

Modern Irish life is conditioned around four to five year political cycles, the yearly budget changes, and ten year capital investment plans few people take very seriously at all, wrapped in the cycles the international economy goes through.

While yearly budgets and ten-year plans are important, if fatally flawed documents, they do miss the *really* big picture, as we move from generation to generation to generation. I will judge this book a success if you, the reader, begin to think seriously about the future and its likely effects on your life. If you decide to make a change to your life based on what you discover in this book – taking out a pension, writing a will, changing the type of house you live in, thinking about starting a new business, travelling more, focusing on preventative health, future-proofing your house, setting up your own business, whatever – the book will have done its job well.

If this book contributes to a public debate, especially on

the issues which will affect us all in the years to come, such as climate change, our economy and its standing in the world, our relationship with Europe, and the changing composition of our population, then I will have shot the moon.

ROBOT MONKEY BUTLERS ARE NOT THE ANSWER

Technology has affected our lives for millennia, from fire and the wheel to the domestication of livestock, public hygiene, antibiotics, cheap fertiliser, the internet, mobile phones, and the new mobile computing devices we are starting to enjoy in vast numbers. The current pace of technical change outstrips that of all previous eras by orders of magnitude, especially in 'high tech' industries (naturally) like information and communications technology, bio-pharmaceuticals and applied electronics. Already in 2009 we live in an era of space tourism, atom-sized robots, quantum teleportation, cheap disposable genetic tests, cars which can break the sound barrier, and medical operations which can attach the arms of a dead man to the body of a living man.

We have vaccines for certain cancers, we have solar cars, personal computers the size of pencil cases, bullet proof wallpaper, insulin chewing gum and cars which can change their body shapes to suit their owners' tastes. And that's today.

Technology is pervasive, but, in many important ways, it changes *nothing*. Yes, in our personal lives, we are more connected than ever, through online social networks, email, Voice Over IP Internet calling and so forth, but for the most important things in your life, you're still there in person.

Yes, the business world moves faster than ever before. Trade is globalised; meaning it occurs between more and more countries, and more often, and outsourcing of many business functions is the future, but business deals still get done face-to-face, over coffee (or a pint), with pens and napkins, winks and nudges, carrots and sticks.

Yes, Ireland is more secular, more individualistic, and slightly less family-oriented as a culture, but look at what happens when a person dies. There are (sometimes) the wake and funeral, there with the mourners sit the friends, there with those who have lost are the priests and other professionals to help. People still have children together, send them to school, and worry about them when they become teenagers.

The basic things don't change that much.

In this book, I'm very keen to stress that technology will *not* solve all our many problems. Robot monkey butlers, should they ever get built, will be brilliant, and I'll be in the queue to buy the first one, but they won't solve Ireland's fundamental issues of producing enough products to survive and thrive in a competitive global marketplace, whilst consuming within our means, long-term, as a society which seeks to help its weaker members, at least some of the time.

Technology, for all its benefits, is only a set of tools – a bag of hammers. What you need is the human expertise to drive the hammer into the nail in the right place in the right wall, again and again and again, to make the building stand up. That expertise, and the ability to conceive of and design a better nail, made of better materials, and profit from the manufacture of that nail, is the way forward. We'll see in this book that the government, by changing targets for numbers of PhD students graduated, and so forth, only move the goal posts of the innovation problem around, when the real crisis (and opportunity for change) is in Ireland's primary and pre-primary schools. The opportunity is to produce people capable of inventing new things. The risk is not producing them. As we'll see, ideas are going to matter more and more in the coming decades. Producing people who can produce those ideas through an educational system fit specifically for that purpose are going to be crucial to our nation's success.

I believe people matter more, and I believe people, at the root, don't change too much. So this book does not harp on about technology, except where it is obvious that technology will change a sphere out of all recognition – and that area is health care, which we can leave until Chapter 9.

People matter more.

Meet the Murphys

I'm far more concerned with the human elements, as I think these are important to discuss in the Ireland of 2050. To illustrate some of the changes I think might happen to the average middle-class family of 2050, I've dreamt up a typical family: the Murphys. Throughout the book, you'll be able to read little vignettes about the family as they prepare to welcome their newest member. You'll also get little 'factoids' in boxes throughout the text, just to spice things up, and get you thinking about the kind of Ireland you might see in your twilight years.

The subtitle of the book is 'how we will be living'. The title and subtitle reflect the focus of the book: rather than presenting a set of 'great, good, average, bad, disaster' scenarios, I've picked what I see as the most likely long-term effects taking place in Irish society, and the world more generally, and I've asked what most people would do in these situations. I think that such a future is, in broad strokes, the one we're on course for, and the future our grandchildren will have to deal with as they become adults.

I'm writing this book for my kids. But, in a certain sense,

I'm also writing this book for their children too, because I want to start a row about the type of country we have today, and the type of country we might end up with, if we put our backs into it. I'll invite you to another row at the end of the book.

Now, before we get started on the history of the future, let's look at the history of the present in Chapter 2, and Ireland's place in the world. It is important for what follows that we have a sense of where we, the Irish people, have come from. Only when we have the context for the present can we think about Ireland in 2050, and our lives in the not-too-distant future.

COFFEE DELIGHT

1 February 2050

Jim Hayes loves his coffee, but that stuff is expensive in 2050. Luckily, he has the kind of pension that lets him spoil himself. Jim retired two years ago, at age seventy.

When he was a teenager in the late 1980s, the price of a coffee was much less, but the choice was quite limited. These days Jim buys locally. Ireland's warm climate makes growing a particularly bitter coffee quite economical. Jim tries to support Irish enterprise when he can. Jim knows his son-in-law is involved in the distribution of the Irish coffee abroad, but doesn't want to ask too many questions about the hows and whys of Jack's businesses. So many of Jack Murphy's ventures have failed since he became married to Jim's daughter, Sarah, that Jim knows not to inquire. Say nothing till you know more, was his late ex-wife's favourite saying.

The coffee leaves Jim refreshed. He returns to his memoir. It is floating in front of him, words and images, movies and songs. It's a little bit like a three-dimensional *Reeling in the Years*, but from a personal perspective. Jim is dipping into his 'life feed' from the 1990s and 2000s, finding old scanned photos of himself at college, his first girlfriend, pictures of him playing hurling, pictures of his first dates with his wife of twenty years, and pictures of his relationships after they split up.

Using these images and sounds, Jim looks back on the Ireland he grew up in, and in many ways, the Ireland he lives in in 2050 is unrecognisable. Dublin, for one, has changed, and changed utterly. 'The country' now means something completely different, because agricultural land overlaps so well with areas previously considered part of the 'urban-rural' divide. Jim thinks over his role in planning and zoning some of these areas as a county councillor, the lack of integration of local priorities with the regional ones, the regional priorities with the national priorities. Ireland's lack of space management and spatial awareness was a fundamental stumbling block to Ireland's economic development and growth, and the rules he helped institute to integrate local planning and zoning with regional and national priorities in a transparent manner did much to change the role of local authorities, and their national counterparts.

Jim feels bittersweet when he thinks about the role he played in the urban/rural debates that began in 2016. He's pretty sure the pressure and stress of his work helped break apart his marriage. For one thing, local interests hampered efforts at a true redesign of the system, because it implied a loss of power at the local level. Jim begins a section on the local/national divide in Irish politics. He writes: 'The dominating feature of Irish politics has been a short-sighted scramble to placate vested interests', but then deletes it, thinking he's written it somewhere else. Jim thinks: It's probably time for another coffee.

2

IRELAND IN THE WORLD

WHERE EXACTLY ARE WE?

Before we can talk about where Ireland might be headed, we
have to get a snapshot of where Ireland is right now, and
where it has just come from. Ireland is not as small as you
might think – it is smaller. The focus of this chapter is to
look at recent Irish history and some current economic and
social problems we are facing, to get a sense of where we
might be heading as a nation in the next forty years. We will
see that Ireland is quite a small place, no matter how you
measure it, that we got here by a combination of luck, hard
work, geography and history. We'll talk about trade and
development, ask how exactly we got here, and discuss some
options for rebuilding the Irish economy. The chapter con-
cludes that, as a country, we will have to make a series of
strategic choices in order to ensure a prosperous future for

Ireland in the world is likely. But first, let's talk about Ireland's size.

SIZE MATTERS

You probably know this, but just in case you don't: we in the Republic of Ireland live on most of an island of around 4.2 million people, sitting on the western edge of Europe. Let's put the numbers in perspective. There are around 4.2 million people in Ireland today. There are close to 67 *thousand* million people alive on Earth. We make up 0.000644ths of the world's population. In terms of landmass, you could fit the island of Ireland into the UK 3.5 times. You could fit Ireland into the USA 137 times.

We are part of the European Union, and have been since 1973. In terms of income, we are one of the richest countries in the world, and richer than many other EU members, despite our recent economic downturn. In terms of wealth, which is stored income, we lag behind the world leaders simply because we have not been rich for very long. We produced around €46,000 worth of stuff (I use 'stuff' in the technical sense) per person in 2008. In 2008, we produced €191 billion worth of stuff in total. While this sounds significant, the total produce of Ireland was less than 1 percent of the total amount produced by the European Union that year.

Let's take a snapshot of modern Ireland with some more or less arbitrary figures[1]. If you were born in Ireland recently, you can expect, on average, to live well into your late seventies or early eighties. Eighty-seven percent of us say we are Catholics; five percent of us say we have no religion at all. Almost everyone in Ireland says they can read the directions on a bottle of medicine. Most of us have mobile phones: in fact, there are 4.4 million mobile phones floating around on this island. For many decades, Ireland was seen as being the 'poorest of the rich', because of its miserable performance as an economy[2]. Not so anymore. Despite the dramatic slowdown in economic activity from 2007 to the present, we are a rich and reasonably well-developed nation on the edge of western Europe.

TRADE AND DEVELOPMENT

Ireland is very dependent on trade with other nations. Three out of the four things we produce in Ireland we try to sell abroad. We sell more abroad than we buy abroad, so our exports (stuff we sell) almost always exceed our imports (stuff we buy). We import oil, gas, electricity, and almost everything else we need to be a modern industrial economy. We are too small to produce much without inputs from abroad.

We export food, beverages, fertilisers, metals, pharmaceuticals, chemicals, computer equipment and software. We trade mainly with the UK, the USA, France, Germany, China and Japan. When these countries experience a recession, they buy less Irish stuff, which can result in a recession here in Ireland if that downturn is long enough.

Ireland has always thrived when trading conditions were good – when other economies had money to spend (and when we were allowed to), Irish exports, especially in agriculture, enriched the nation. The path of economic and societal development in Ireland must necessarily follow the turbulence of international economic movements, such as the downturn the world economy experienced in 2007, 2008 and 2009.

As I write these words, we in Ireland are experiencing the

worst economic slowdown of any developed nation in the world. Demand for Irish stuff is going down. People all over the world are buying less, selling less, and businesses in Ireland are letting people go, or going under themselves. Our financial services sector suffered great losses, thanks to the perfect storm of a collapsing international economy – which reduced the sector's ability to borrow to finance its debts – combined with the implosion of the construction bubble, to which many of the financial sectors' debts were issued. Unemployment, once thought by the Irish public to have been conquered, has returned in force. More than 400,000 people from a workforce of only 1,800,000 are now unemployed at the time of writing. The numbers of those unemployed are projected to rise to nearly 500,000 people by the end of 2009.

The Irish government relied heavily on property-related taxes to supplement reduced income tax levels, and so when these taxes were gone, the government found itself needing to borrow heavily to finance current government spending.

Under increasing pressure from an enraged electorate, the government must make political concessions to powerful interest groups (for example, the reversal of medical card benefits for the elderly, subsidies for employers' groups, and so on), while simultaneously trying to take the necessary steps to return Ireland to economic prosperity.

The key steps the government needs to take are to increase income taxes, broaden the tax base (meaning that more people at lower levels of income are going to start paying tax), reduce public expenditure by reducing the size and scope of the public service, and try to rein in spending on capital projects like roads and ports.

The problem is made worse because rising unemployment costs the government twice – in social welfare payments and in lost taxes – and so, to curb spending, the government needs to help create new jobs. Creating jobs efficiently is not going to be easy. The economy desperately needs new businesses in order to create new jobs. But these businesses can't get seed capital to start, because banks won't lend to them. We have an unsolvable logical dilemma, a catch-22. As I've written above, we are experiencing a perfect economic storm, and that is where we are as I write these words – in the middle of that storm.

How exactly did we get here?

The origin and dramatic nature of the turnaround in Ireland's economic fortunes is a reminder that all good things do come to an end, and that periods of growth are followed by periods of retrenchment, which are then followed by periods of rebuilding.

The slump we are experiencing in 2009 and 2010 comes after an explosive expansion in the fortunes of Ireland's economy dating from the late 1980s, now called the Celtic Tiger. In 1986, for example, nearly 18 percent of the workforce was unemployed. Getting a business loan would have cost you nearly 20 percent of the principal in interest.

Emigration was a fact of life for many young Irish people before 1990. During the Celtic Tiger, the synergy of an increased demand for Irish products in the Eurozone following the completion of the Single European Market, combined with a buoyant US economy, billions of euros of EU structural funds to upgrade our infrastructure, and the presence of multinational companies drawn to Ireland by low corporation taxes combined with a highly educated, young workforce, thanks to free third-level education and the baby-boomer generation maturing, all merged in lock-step to increase economic output. The increase in economic output created a demand for more workers, which brought more women into the labour force, brought a generation of Irish emigrants home, and started the process of bringing new immigrants to Ireland.

As a nation, we saw increasing household incomes and living standards throughout the Celtic Tiger period. In fact, we saw a doubling of living standards from the early 1990s until 2002, with very little inflation – a remarkable achievement which some have called an economic miracle. I would be one of those people. All in all, the Tiger years *were* a miracle. Increased economic activity began to churn and change Irish society, reshaping what the average Irish person expected in terms of their personal productivity, their private wealth and their standard of living. The Tiger years changed, and changed utterly, the status of women in Irish society by bringing more women into the labour force, giving them economic freedom and opportunities for personal advancement and equality, which further eroded the influence of the Catholic Church, especially with regard to contraception and divorce. Thanks to the Celtic Tiger, the 'spectre of emigration' had gone[3]. The children of the 1990s were the first generation of Irish people since the 1840s who did not have to emigrate in large numbers for purely economic reasons.

I don't wish to dwell too long on it, but certainly another very important force during this period was the peace process in Northern Ireland. Though not directly related to the Celtic Tiger years, the peace process clearly underpinned them. It is difficult to underestimate the long-term social, political, psychological and cultural significance of the creation of a relatively peaceful society, following a protracted sectarian conflict. The peace process did, does and will pay an economic dividend to the citizens of the Republic and the subjects of Northern Ireland.

The Tiger years also brought a wave of multiculturalism to Ireland, as economic migrants from the EU's accession countries and elsewhere sought jobs and better lives here, forming their own communities, businesses and diasporas. The challenges of how best to integrate Irish culture with the cultures of these new entrants are ones future generations will face. As part of the European Union, Ireland must now, technically, allow for the free movement in and out of its territory of 450 million people, and this fact alone will change the face of modern, post-industrial Ireland. Increasing the integration of different countries will have effects, partly as a result of the boom years, and partly because the children of the baby boomers – those born in the 1950s and 1960s – are having children of their own. We are currently seeing a large increase in the fertility rate in Ireland; this will have large-scale effects in the 2030s and 2050s as each new generation emerges. In the last census, the young, productive tranche of the Irish population (twenty- to forty-five-year-olds) accounted for 38 percent of the total population. As these people (and I'm one of them) mature and have children themselves, the likely effects on Irish society will be vast. Those effects are the subject of this book.

The Tiger years ended largely in 2002, when export-led growth was largely replaced by a boom in the construction sector. Increased numbers in employment, making more money, and expecting to make yet more in the future, meant that people wanted to buy houses. This kicked off a spiral of wage increases, which led to more houses being built, which led to more jobs in construction. The process was unsustainable, and faltered in 2007, as the international credit crunch forced a re-evaluation of the overhang of houses already constructed. This reacted with the inability of sellers to find buyers willing to pay more and more for new houses. Around 15 percent of the economy's overall production in 2008 was just construction-related[4].

REBUILDING: WHAT WE NEED IS AN ACCIDENT

Ireland is too small to prop its faltering economy up by selling things we produce here to ourselves, or by asking the government to step in and fill the space left by receding markets. Strategically, if we want to get richer, as a country we need to produce goods and services the world wants to buy. The route to doing this is to create a basis for trade in high-value, export-oriented, home-grown products and services. Such businesses that survive and thrive will grow the economy, and Irish society with them, through exports, producing what is known as export-led growth.

The logic behind export-led growth is that if the stuff Irish people sell is more attractive in terms of price and quality than other countries' stuff, Irish sellers will see orders for their stuff increasing, meaning that the economy will grow over time due to this increased economic activity. Better products produced in Ireland and sold abroad means a richer Ireland. The only problem with this strategy is that it can't be institutionalised to a large degree – successes like these are a matter of luck[5], of trial and error. The old English proverb 'There's many a slip 'twixt the cup and the lip' applies when it comes to the development of any nation. Plans and strategies are fine, but when it comes to economic development, and economic miracles, most of what occurs is by accident –

the Celtic Tiger being a case in point. I believe, and I'm not alone in this belief, that the Tiger years happened as the conflation of a series of very fortunate circumstances, rather than as a result of any grand design by policymakers. The subsequent downturn in the economy is, likewise, due to the actions of many individual actors in the process, rather than one or two groups. So we need luck if our hard work is to succeed. Joe Lee[6] puts it better than most, when talking of the prospects for a national recovery for Ireland in the 1980s:

> Such a leap forward may still occur . . . If such transformation occurs, however, it will not have been the result of foresight. It will be a sheer accident.

It is telling that the same issues of foresight and transformation strike at the heart of our public discourse today, thirty years on.

Answering the Global Question

Because of its size, Ireland is unable to have any significant positive or negative effect on the functioning of the world economy. As I showed earlier, whether we double our wealth, or halve it, it means nothing to the international economic community. We are just too small. The change in our fortunes, of course, affects us in Ireland. This is the key to Ireland's global question: what we do will not affect those outside Ireland unduly, but what *they* do could harm us with relative ease.

We've seen that the wealth of the Irish economy will increasingly come from external sources, so Ireland is very vulnerable to large swings in the world economy, such as the negative swing in economic activity we are experiencing right now. Larger nations can wield enough political, cultural and economic clout through their large governments to change, or even reverse, some of the effects of large-scale economic downturns, by spending their way out of recessions and borrowing to do so. Ireland cannot.

Ireland's place in the world, and the well-being of its citizens, is dependent on how we manage the challenges a globalised world will present to us in the future. Many studies place Ireland at the forefront of globalised nations[7].

Globalisation is a term which means many things to many people but can be roughly defined as the increased integration and interdependence between markets and economies. The effects of globalisation are increased movement (and interaction) between countries of goods, services, information, ideas, and, of course, people. The world has experienced waves of globalisation several times, most notably from 1870 to 1913[8].

The successive waves of globalisation were beneficial to Ireland as a trading nation, when we were positioned to take advantage of these waves. The current wave of globalisation does not seem to have adversely affected Ireland – although imports are dropping, the channels through which this trade occurs are not being shut off by 'protectionist' policies.

Economist Michael O'Sullivan[9] has written about Ireland's potential answer to what he calls 'the global question': can Ireland maintain its sovereignty and still manage its affairs in the context of powerful, highly integrated international markets in which it will almost certainly not be a key player? The global question is an extension of the national question Eamon De Valera posed to the Irish people: can we maintain our sense of ourselves in the face of powerful external forces?

There is no simple answer to the global question, but one possible set of answers leads to a recognition that the balance of economic, military, and political power in the world may be changing. Many, many studies have pointed to the resurgent Chinese and Indian economies[10], noting a shift in political and economic power from the West – the US and the EU – to the East, notably China, India and Japan. The thinking goes that these new players will change the stakes, and the rules, of the how the game of geopolitics is played. Don't believe the hype.

ORIENTATION, GEOGRAPHY AND TRADE

People who think about the future a lot tend to extrapolate out trends they can see working in the world at the moment. A slightly longer view of the past gives grounds for questioning whether the current rapid growth we are witnessing in countries like China and India will persist. For example, as discussed earlier, in the 1980s it was fashionable to portray Japan as the successor to the USA's position as the global economic powerhouse. Policymakers in the eighties were urged to adopt Japanese-style institutions and employers were encouraged to adopt work practices along Japanese lines. The Japanese, it was felt, were gearing up to surpass the United States, because their productivity was so much higher than that of the US. The dismal record of Japan in the 1990s, however, shows that today's hot ticket may not be quite so hot in ten years' time. Forceful statements about China's resurgence to the contrary, the study of history is a reminder that this too shall pass.

Notions that the US economy is in a period of long-term decline are misplaced[11]. The United States is economically, militarily and politically the most powerful country in the world. The country's spending on defence alone is five times the entire output of Ireland – and their spending on defence is almost as much as all other nations' spending in this area combined. 26 percent of all the world's economic activity took place in the US last year.

My point in this section is simple: too many things would have to go spectacularly wrong before the US loses its position as the world's pre-eminent power. Critics point first to the decline of US manufacturing, and particularly of the steel and auto industries. But the critics made the same points in the 1970s, 1980s and 1990s. Critics point to US energy security, and argue that US oil shortages will undermine the economy. But a quick look at the numbers dispels that notion. The US produced 8.3 million barrels of oil a day in 2006. It produces more oil than Iran, Kuwait or the United Arab Emirates. The US is one of the world's largest energy producers. The US does import vast quantities of oil and gas, but given the scale of production that takes place there, that makes sense.

Critics point to the greying of US society relative to the rest of the world. True again, but they don't talk about just how much space there is in the USA. In terms of population density, the world average is 49 people per square kilometre. Ireland's population density is 62 people per square kilometre, Japan's is 341 and Germany's is 237. The United States' population density is only 34[12]. There is a lot of room to grow and, in fact, the US is largely under-populated. The US economy has plenty of spare land (and natural resources), plenty of labour, and plenty of capital – all three prerequisites of economic growth.

Many analysts points to the rise of the Chinese economy as a sign that power will shift eastward. I don't think China can become a rival to the US in the medium term, because China's growth over the last thirty years, while spectacular, does not mean its growth will carry on forever. Far from it. The fact that China has been growing so quickly for so long actually diminishes the likelihood that it will continue this ferocious pace of development. But to see why, you have to look at China's geography and history. The majority of China's billion citizens live quite close to the sea (less than 1,000 miles away). Much of the rest of the country is actually under-populated, and very poor.

The history of China can be written as the struggle between the poor peasants in the interior of China, and their richer cousins who live near the coasts. Throughout China's history, as trade between the coasts and the rest of the world has increased, massive inequalities in wealth between regions have repeatedly caused political instability, which has occasionally led to revolution. The opening up of the Chinese economy to trade since the death of Mao has been controlled, but the internal forces built up by the increase of wealth in the cities relative to the rural regions is, if anything, more pronounced than before. The redistribution of resources from the wealthy regions to the poorer ones creates tensions which become exacerbated in hard times, as unemployment soars and bad debts increase; these factors foment social, economic and political instability. Something will cause the familiar fault lines to crack in China over the next forty years to 2050. Remember that Japan was the growth story in the 1980s. Remember that the Celtic Tiger was once seen as a model of how small economies could lift themselves out of poverty. To those who champion China's ascendance to the world stage, I'd respectfully ask them to look at their history books. This too shall pass.

I know what you're thinking: what has this little jaunt

into cartoon geopolitics to do with Ireland? Let me answer that question now.

STRATEGIC CHOICES: POINT WEST OR EAST?

Ireland must make a choice. Does it orient itself to the West, to the US and Europe, or does it open itself up to the East? There is a trade-off to be made here. Given the balance of probabilities, I would argue that Ireland should exert itself in the direction of the West, and continue the policies of Seán Lemass and Jack Lynch, rather than courting new markets in the East exclusively.

That's not to say that we shouldn't trade with India or China; far from it. Individual Irish enterprises will seek the highest gain they think they can get, and if that means investing in China, then great, I'm all for that. My point concerns the broad strategy Ireland should follow, rather than the decision of a firm, or even a sector. Going back to Joe Lee[13]:

> Small states must rely on the quality of their strategic thinking to counter their vulnerability to international influences. Without superior strategic thinking, they will be buffeted rudderless, like a cork on a wave. It is virtually impossible for a small country to 'plan' in a rigorous sense. This is all the more reason to devise a strategy that will help one respond coherently, rather than epileptically, to changing circumstances.

This is a slight digression, but here's one vision for such a strategy.

Understanding our geography and history, as well as our size, means that we will have to go with the ebbs and flows of the political tide. We straddle the divide between the US and western Europe, and can connect the two. There really isn't much of a conflict between the US and the EU, but when matters of disagreement do arise, the Irish position should be tacitly to favour the US side, rather than the EU side, of any argument, while agreeing in principle with the EU. This is because we are already part of the EU, yet we trade more and more with the US.

The nation's strategy must be to increase our connections with the US, above all else. We need to make it easier to trade in vast quantities with the US and other rich nations. To do so, we can take advantage of US dominance of the sea, our historical openness to trade, and our geography. The establishment of a supertanker port in the next ten years is a national priority, as is the development of roads and rail links across Ireland to accommodate industrial quantities of freight. Spending on large capital projects for the foreseeable future should go up, not down, in spite of our current economic situation. Ireland is ideally placed to allow super tankers to sail across the Atlantic ocean, depositing their cargoes into smaller ships to be sent to Europe, and sending goods on to companies located in Ireland for further processing if necessary. We can have true deep-water ports to create a trade hub off the west coast of Ireland. This is just one example of a national strategy to follow.

This chapter was about showing where Ireland has come from, showing how we came through the Celtic Tiger years into the era of a post-construction boom and its attendant dilemmas. The way forward, I feel, is to link ourselves as a trading hub to the US economy by enhancing our infrastructure in order to take advantage of the dominant position of the world's largest economy.

FAMILY AFFAIRS

9 March 2050

Jack Murphy's parents split up when he was seven, in 2016. The stress of the breakup is still with Jack, and he thinks about his relationship with his father today – how it has changed from his teenaged years. Jack thinks the counselling he went through as a teenager helped somewhat, but really, it was his friends who got him through. When Jack was at school, most of the children in his class had parents who were divorced, remarried, or in the process of getting a divorce. It was commonplace, and the school system became fairly good at offering services to children like Jack to help them cope.

Jack worries about Maeve. He knows her pregnancy, combined with her schoolwork, is tiring her, and her now non-existent relationship with her boyfriend, and soon to be new father, is upsetting her. He makes a note to talk with her this weekend about growing up with only one parent around, and how he coped, adapted, and ultimately thrived. He hopes the talk will help.

FACTOID: Today's investments in green business solutions will take off in four to five years. Governments are likely to take serious steps to curb global warming about the same time as the impacts of climate change on rich nations become more extreme. Driven by the profit motive and heavily subsidised by governments around the world, entrepreneurs are working on alternative energy sources such as wind turbines, biofuels, nuclear plants and solar cells. This entire 'green revolution' is growing by 30 to 50 percent per year – roughly the same rate as the famous Moore's Law, which states that the power and speed of information technologies will double every two years. Today, green technology is roughly a $500 billion market, and is expected to reach $10 trillion in 2020 – larger than autos, health care and defence.

The twin problems we face at present, centring on energy generation and environmental protection, actually offer opportunities for personal profit and profound societal change. It may be that the resulting economic growth in a noble cause to protect the Earth could even defuse the race towards conflict and the development of weapons of mass destruction, as diverse cultures are more closely integrated into the global community. Almost all sectors of the economy are likely to be rejuvenated with high-tech advances in roughly the same time-frame. A new wave of green autos powered by hybrid, electric and fuel-cell engines should enter the mainstream about 2013 to 2018, and we are likely to see 'intelligent cars', which may even drive themselves. This green revolution is likely to come primarily from the USA, because of its current technological superiority.

3

THE DIVORCE BOMB: OUR FAMILIES, OUR KIDS AND OUR CULTURE

THE DIVORCE BOMB, THE DEATH OF FEMINISM, AND IRISH FAMILIES

If you're in a relationship, and it's having problems, marriage won't solve them. On a ten-point scale of happiness, with 1 indicating too-miserable-to-breathe, and 10 indicating at-the-point-of-orgasm happy, recent research[1] has found that people expect that marriage will make a difference of four or five points, whereas the real difference between married subjects and subjects who never married is about 0.1.

In modern societies like ours, the 'happiness effect' of marriage seems to be temporary: about five years into the marriage, happiness returns to its pre-marriage level. Other longitudinal studies suggest that the causality may well go the other way: in other words, people who are happy in their marriage seem to have been happier before they were married. Those who were miserable before they were married returned to their misery only a few short months after the wedding.

So: if you're miserable now, putting on a ring will only help temporarily. Buy yourself something nice instead, or do some sit-ups. Marriage isn't the answer.

Rates of divorce in Ireland are starting to increase. Almost twelve thousand couples have now been granted divorces by Irish courts since it was legalised in 1997. Fairly soon it is likely that we will see one in three of the marriages which began in the 2000s break up[2]. The institutions of marriage and family are intimately connected in Ireland as they are in many other countries, so a rising divorce rate, coupled with an increased number of children being born, creates the potential for societal shifts we have seen in other countries. Without trying to sound apocalyptic, the rise of so-called 'broken' families will have large impacts on Ireland's economy and society, as it has in other countries like the UK and USA. To take one example, research has found that children of divorcees don't do as well in school as children from 'stable' marriages, they are more prone to bouts of depression, and they tend to struggle when forming new long-term relationships when adults themselves. Divorce, or the death of a spouse, substantially increases the chances of ill-health in adults, even when they remarry. Though there is actually no consensus on the long-term effects of divorce on children, it can be said that the explosion of a divorce bomb, along with a large increase in the population of children, will have both positive and negative effects on Ireland by 2050. Divorce has environmental effects as well: cohabiting couples and families around the globe use resources more efficiently than households that have split up. Researchers have calculated that, in 2005, divorced American households used between 42 and 61 percent more resources per person than before they separated, spending 46 percent more per person on electricity and 56 percent more on water.

People who describe themselves as being of no religion are more likely to be divorced or separated[3]. More than 7 percent of those of no religion have experienced marital breakdown, higher than the 4.6 percent figure for Catholics, or 6.8 percent for other Christians. As the influence of the Catholic Church wanes, decimated by repeated scandals, it is reasonable to assume their sanctions against divorce will hold less and less sway for an increasingly secular Irish population.

As women's participation and importance in the work-force increases, in particular, reaching the same levels of income, position, and status as men, a tectonic shift has taken place in attitudes regarding domestic work. There's nothing new here, we have been aware of this change for many years. However, this could lead to a reappraisal of the role of men in the upbringing of children, changing the norm that the woman usually receives custody of the child in a divorce case. Michael Kimmel, author of *The Gendered Society*[4], has claimed that school-aged children who do housework with their fathers are more likely to get along with their peers, and have more friends. Looking forward to 2050, it's easy to imagine a Father's Day gift being something simple, like breakfast in bed, and all Dad's chores done for him for the day. He might also like some chocolates. The average father in the US now spends about three hours inter-acting with his school-aged children per weekend day, up significantly from estimates in earlier decades. At the same time, a father's interactions with their children remain shaped by older expectations about what men and women should do.

A FAMILY AFFAIR

The family is one of the most stable elements in Irish society, and it is through the family that children have tradition-
ally been raised. Ireland's children are currently experiencing
the fundamental changes taking place in Irish society: as we
get richer, and work more, our relationships with our children are changing. A recent study[5] found that one in four
nine-year-olds are overweight; 18 percent of nine-year-olds
live in a single-parent family; and 61 percent of mothers, and
43 percent of fathers, felt that they had missed out on home
or family activities (that they would otherwise have liked to
take part in) because of their work commitments. With the
increase in women's participation in the world of work and
the equality movement which sprang up to protect women's
interests, the need for a woman to be married to ensure security of income is gone. Current divorce laws in Ireland and
around the developed world now provide for financial security for the rearing of children in the event of a marital breakdown.

Families will still be common in 2050, but you might not
recognise them. No more husband, wife and 2.1 kids as the
norm. The isolated, socially-distant nuclear family of the
1950s was really an anomaly. Most of the time, families have
looked slightly different, with more care-giving to the elderly and weaker members of the family, and more interaction
with the community. The institution of the family has shifted and changed many times: it is the most adaptable institution. I don't think families will go away, but the notion of the
'average' Irish family surely will.

Many of the biggest changes in the next century, at least
in the developed world, will be driven by the demographic

tilt away from children and towards the elderly. A snapshot of a family gathering in 2050 will show lots of gray hair, and not too many nappies. Even now, for the first time in history, the average German, the average American and the average Japanese has more parents living than children. The family will take centre stage again in the provision of eldercare, especially among the poor, with state and private supports in the community.

It is important to remember that forty years is a pretty long time – almost anything can happen. A long-term economic decline in Ireland, coupled with an explosion in health care needs by older citizens, could force more people to depend on families instead of the state, in fact returning us partially to the situation which prevailed in the 1950s and before. A religious revival could restore traditional mores, returning the Catholic Church to its pre-eminent position in Irish cultural life. And a revised calculation of rational interest in light of social chaos could call the benefits of extreme individualism into question. We've already seen that a demographic-economic crisis could invoke all three of these mechanisms.

The idea that marriage was the key to a 'nuclear' family – husband, wife, 2.1 children – is wrong. Marriage in Ireland is still seen by many as the route to a happy, stable life. In previous eras, marriage was society's keystone institution. It provided many things to each participant: companionship, social status, sexual opportunities, the chance to have children, and care-giving for older relatives and friends. For women in particular, marriage provided security of income and assurances of continued well-being for their children. The more children you had, the more likely you were to have a continued and easy retirement. There were no downsides to having as many children as you could. Not so today. Now the cost of having children (in terms of time foregone as well as money lost) is quite high, and with more and more children being born to 'single' parents[6], this limits the number of children being born as well. Things are changing: in 1980, one in twenty births took place outside marriage, but today one in three do. That trend is set to continue. Births out of marriage are going to exceed births in marriage for the first time in Irish society by 2012, and though there has been a spike in the number of marriages as the Pope's children get older, the surge in births happened *before* the surge in marriages. 'Lone parent' families are becoming the norm, with marriage often simply an option for people in their thirties, with children.

Marriage has lost the two most powerful 'pull' factors it once possessed: the promise of economic security for themselves and their children, and as a socially acceptable place to raise children. Now people marry for pleasure, for love, or for social status, but it is rarely the case that a couple 'need' to stay together any more, especially in the longer run.

Ironically, despite our new-found secular and sexual freedoms, given the harsh economic climate we are currently facing, and the numbers of children being born at the moment, we may see couples staying together out of a traditional economic need. But once the economy recovers, and these couples and their children grow older, I think we will see a boom in divorces by 2020, with perhaps half or more of all couples separating by then.

Remember: the majority of women will have been working for four generations by 2050, with equality of opportunity and financial security. If a marriage dissolves, divorce will be nothing to fear. The money and house will hopefully be divided equally without the need for an expensive divorce lawyer. Most divorced women will sail happily along with no great financial worries, and no social stigma attached to their new status.

Opponents of divorce point to the very low numbers of divorces taking place in Ireland relative to other countries. I believe this is because of the cultural power the Catholic Church held for the average divorcee of our generation, and generations past. They were raised in a culture where the authority of the institutional church was not questioned, and that fact, coupled with the wide range of mediating options like compulsory marriage counselling and legal separations, means that the impact of the 1997 legislation on divorce has not been felt – yet.

The cultural hold of the Catholic Church as an institution of power has been declining since the late 1960s, when the church's ban on contraception was widely broken by its members, beginning in the late 1960s[7]. The assaults on the church's power have continued ever since. It is very difficult to see anything but a gradual decline for the Catholic Church, and ultimately a complete separation of the church from the state, which began in 1972 when the special status of the Catholic Church was removed from the Constitution.

For many years, the Catholic Church acted as a shadow welfare state, providing education, employment, and social welfare assistance of a kind, and doing many good works. The church also abused its power in many ways, and the public's recoil over the revelations of the extent of these abuses will see the church's power disappear almost completely. Ireland will become a largely secular nation in practice, even if, for at least two more generations, the majority of us (and our children) will remain nominally Catholic.

OUR KIDS: LET'S NOT KILL THEIR CREATIVITY. KILL THE EDUCATIONAL SYSTEM INSTEAD.

Children starting school this year will start retiring in the 2070s. Nobody has any idea how to educate them for a future, which, in fairness, we can't properly foresee. Education is supposed to be the vehicle by which our children will prosper in the future. Children have extraordinary capacities for innovation, for creativity, and for change. It is very hard to find someone today who thinks the educational experience we give our children doesn't to some degree squander their talents and capacities, by shoehorning children into a particular form of learning by doing, and learning by rote.

The student becomes adept, as Richard Hoggart[8] writes, at

> a technique of apparent learning, of acquiring facts. He learns how to receive a purely literate education, one using only a small part of his personality and challenging only a limited area of his being. He begins to see life as a ladder, as a permanent examination with some praise and some further exhortation at each stage. He becomes an expert imbiber and doler-out; his competence will vary, but will rarely be accompanied by genuine enthusiasm. He rarely feels the reality of knowledge, of other men's thoughts and imaginings, on his own pulses; he rarely discovers an author for himself and on his own. In this half of life he can respond only if there is a direct connection with the system of training. He has something of the blinkered pony about him; sometimes he is trained by those who have been through the same regimen, who are hardly unblinkered themselves, and who praise him in the degree to which he takes comfortably to their blinders.

Think of all the educational systems in the world. Generally speaking, the same hierarchy dominates: science and maths on top, languages a distant second, the arts a very distant third. Today, the extent to which our children succeed in Ireland is the extent to which they conform to an outdated notion of 'academic ability' built around this hierarchy. We prepare our children for their lives as adults by attempting, in some sense, to produce university professors, at the expense of every other aspect of their lives. There's a reason for this: the educational system is built to meet the needs of industry, to prepare our kids for a type of nine-to-five work which is currently dying out, and which will not be the dominant form of industrial organisation in rich countries by the middle of this century.

There is an intertwining of religious belief, the need for skilled workers to facilitate economic expansion, and efficiency. Educators in the US were being told as early as 1912 that 'the schools as well as other institutions must submit to the test of efficiency'. The call for efficiency was heard, and obeyed, in Irish schools as well.

Today, we want our best graduates to be mathematically and scientifically literate, because these are the languages of industry and science – the drivers of our future growth, so the story goes. The types of subjects we lionise, and the way we cultivate these types of intelligence, is wrong, because it presupposes that the work requirements of the future will be similar to those of the present, when we are all pretty sure that the future will be radically different[9].

We don't teach our children how to deal with uncertainty, how to deal with complexity, or how to be creative. We teach them how to regurgitate, how to seek certainty, how to hand back the 'right' answers, regardless of whether they understand the method through which the answer happens to arrive. And, in their wisdom, when they have the choice, students turn away from the subjects most heavily associated with regurgitation towards other, more interesting, subjects. Ironically, mathematics and science subjects suffer because of this, and our strategic national priorities are put at risk as a result.

I am thirty-one years old, and I work in education. I have *never* met anyone who described the Leaving Certificate as anything but a trial, an ordeal, a ring of fire to be passed through and then quickly forgotten. Unmanageable expectations about a particular type of performance in a particularly useless type of activity – list learning – deform an individual's creativity, bend the educational establishment to achieve these expectations, and change parents' behaviours with their children. Everything is competitive. I am not against competition, when the prize is worth the game being played, and when the players themselves aren't damaged by the game. In the case of our educational system, however, I feel that we are not doing most of our students justice. The ones who happen to be gifted at memorising or mathematics are rewarded with coveted and prestigious places at university and, thereafter, with lucrative, rewarding careers. The students whose range of abilities falls outside the strangled remit of the Leaving Certificate are left to find another path. Some do; others don't.

Of course, you can find examples where one person succeeded wildly despite a lack of formal education. But you can find many more examples where individuals without formal education have failed to meet their potential. The truth is that in the aggregate, those with qualifications will do better than those without. 'Successes' and 'failures' – both groups of people are harmed by the experience. The notion that the Leaving Certificate is a true learning experience, that it in any sense adds value to someone who goes through it, is a joke.

Intelligence is diverse. Intelligence is visual, auditory, kinetic, dynamic and interactive. If the challenges we will face in the future are dependent on harnessing new ideas, then the people with the best new ideas will command a wage premium in the international marketplace for jobs. It is an economic and social imperative that we should wish to foster intelligence, to let someone's abilities grow and develop.

Sir Ken Robinson, a leader in the field of educational reform, writes[10]:

> The world is changing faster than ever in our history. Our best hope for the future is to develop a new paradigm of human capacity to meet a new era of human existence. We need to evolve a new appreciation of the importance of nurturing human talent along with an understanding of how talent expresses itself differently in every individual. We need to create environments – in our schools, in our workplaces, and in public offices – where every person is inspired to grow creatively.

We want the labour market to reward intelligence and creativity, and it does: the people with the brightest ideas do seem to do very well for themselves. Creativity is the process of having original ideas. The educational system as it stands embeds a fear of not having the right answer to a question, or not showing the correct steps to achieving a solution, through the examination process. Those who copy down the correct answer or memorise the set of steps do well in exams, and are rewarded. Those who don't, aren't. In the real world, there is no 'right' answer, and you don't know the steps to take to get to the solution. In fact, you spend most of the time trying to come up with the right question in the first place. So we prepare our students for a role which they shouldn't perform, and because those roles are not well paid, they will not make the individual better off, and because society is the sum of the individuals within it, society is not made better off, either. The truly useful parts of the Leaving Certificate are its analytic, language, and art components, but the science and maths curricula must change, as recent reports from government bodies have argued, and to some effect[11]. One of the central theses of this book is that we can change the future by acting today. A stitch in time duly saves nine. By changing the educational experience of our children, we can change the adults they turn into, and so change the range of options those adults are exposed to, and they can then pass their increased wealth and improved living standards onto their children, who in turn will reap the rewards of an enlightened and creative approach to education, and so on. It's important to restate this basic message, and to note that a stratified, one-size-fits-all approach to education must always marginalise those students who don't take naturally to learning the way the teachers want them to learn. So something vital is lost, at great personal cost and, eventually, at great cost to society too.

Assuming a healthy population, education is the key to maintaining high living standards for that population into the future. As we will see in Chapter 7, because the world of work and the demand for foreign workers will be changing rapidly into the 2030s, as the composition of the US workforce begins to grey more rapidly, children born today will be well positioned to take advantage of the high wages and investment opportunities which a US economy will give them. That is, if – and it's a big if – we prepare our children for the types of jobs US firms might need in twenty or forty years' time. We will explore the changes to the world of work in Chapter 7 more fully, but for now, let's say that work practices will shift in several ways. Employees will work in more decentralised, specialised firms, and employer/employee relationships will become less standardised and more individualised, because individuals will have more power over their terms and conditions as employees. Money earned abroad but spent locally will enrich the Irish economy immensely into the future.

The benefits of fostering creativity are not just a higher wage for the individual who happens to be a bit more creative than everyone else. Because they might make something which other people might like, creative individuals perform a productive, profitable and transformative function in society by creating jobs, new products, and new ways for society to see itself. Companies which are primarily creative in nature tend to be small and prone to failure – most people's ideas, frankly, suck. When an idea does strike gold, though – say, the idea of indexing the World Wide Web, coupled to a simple, searchable interface – the founders of the idea make billions, and society changes as a result. Most creative enterprises fail, but the benefits of success are immense. This is why we need to teach our children to accept failure of an idea: as long as the idea fails constructively, it should be viewed as preparation for the next attempt. Children who are taught that it is fine to fail will embrace uncertainty and complexity in a different way. Some of these children will have brilliant ideas which will change their lives, the face of Irish society and the world at large, if we let them. We have to change the educational system to build in this tolerance for failure, creativity and experimentation if we want our children to succeed in the future. In short, kill the educational system we have, not our kids' creativity.

CREATIVITY KILLED THE CAT, BUT MADE REALLY COOL HANDBAGS

1 April 2050

Bobby Murphy is building a cat in class for a modelling project. He is thinking about the skeleton, the muscle tissue, the range of movement, the physics of how cats move. Much of the brute computation is, of course, done for him, but Bobby is a numerate young man, and likes solving some of these problems by hand. Then he gets an idea. Famous people love animals. Famous people love handbags and accessories. Why not engineer a few pockets for accessories inside the cat?

Bobby gets to work, building a clasp of bone and two skin pouches for the cat/handbag mashup. His friends join in, and soon the class has a range of cat, dog, and rabbit accessories, in different colours, sizes, and shapes, as April Fool's products. Someone mentions using wirelessly enabled snail shells as earrings. Someone else thinks about sending the project files to another class who are studying fabrication and 3-D printing, but Bobby's instructor stops them – it's lunchtime.

DIGITAL NATIVES WON'T CARE ABOUT PRIVACY

While you are online, everything about you is saved. A future is coming where your actions online will be recorded, your movements will be tracked, and your conversations will no longer be fleeting. This is a future brought to you not by some *1984*-like dystopia, but by the natural tendencies of computers to produce data. Increasingly, our actions and statements are not lost, but are recorded, stored and analysed, perhaps for profit and power. Sometimes, recording information about yourself is desirable, since it can create a convenient way for you to remember things you might otherwise have forgotten. But in practice it is rarely you who is doing the recording. In a perfect world, we would each choose how much personal data to show to the world, based on how much we value the services that use our personal data.

To take one example, advertising is a modern annoyance that could in principle be made less annoying if advertisers could adopt a more targeted approach. Part of the reason advertising is annoying is that most of the ads we see are not remotely interesting to us. Enter the miracle of personal data: if only advertisers knew enough about our real interests, they would know which ads were not relevant to us individually, and would show us only ads that we were interested in seeing! The argument doesn't really wash, but there is a key notion here: that a trade-off must be made between living online, and so being monitored, and living offline, and retaining a significant degree of privacy.

Your grandchildren will be part of a globally connected culture. Your children's children will be part of a networked public, their identities formed, spun out – and shed – online. We are failing to prepare our children for the lives they will lead online, because we have no idea what those online lives will look like. They just haven't been invented yet.

We *can* teach our children the skills they will need to navigate the flows of information to which they will be exposed throughout their lives. But, largely speaking, we don't. For the majority of today's teenagers – the first, half-formed batch of 'digital natives' the world has ever seen – we allow them to learn the rules of engagement with the digital world for themselves, alone in their bedrooms, and perhaps amongst their friends. There is no structure to their learning, and as a result digital literacy will be a hit-and-miss affair. Those with the natural abilities, opportunities and resources to pick up the basic skills needed to handle the complexity of information will prosper.

Those unlucky enough to be without these gifts will flounder, and their lives will be poorer as a result. We can change the outcome for these children by acting today. Let me explain why we should act today, and decisively, to teach our children how to understand, mediate, produce and disseminate information online. Many people in Ireland have no regular access to high-speed internet services, even in school, although they will increasingly be able to have internet-ready content delivered to their phones. This has major social implications, because the children of the rich will have access to these online resources more often than the children of the poor.

Think about infants today, born in 2009. They will be the young adults of 2025, and the middle-aged of 2050. Before they were born, their ultrasound pictures were taken, and perhaps shared online with their parents' friends. When they were born, the baby's proud parents posted pictures of the newborn on their blog, or their social-network page. From before birth through to their first steps, their first day at school, their first friendships, sporting outings, social occasions, birthday parties, funny mishaps, personal successes and personal failures, their first use of mobile phones, through to their teenage years, today's children have been digitally 'tattooed' by their parents. Once the children of 2009 acquire the right to mediate their own online presence, through a social network of their own (tied, most likely, to a school or social group the child belongs to in the physical world), the notion of a digital tattoo goes away, replaced by the information about themselves the child chooses to place in an archived, searchable record which potential partners and employers can access whenever they want to.

Researchers[12] have coined the term 'life feed' to describe the cumulative digital record of a life, from birth to death, which is played out and stored online. Our children will routinely give up control of the information they produce, and parts of their identity, for the speed and convenience with which a digital profile provides them.

Privacy issues abound. But these privacy issues are *our* issues. Our notion of privacy is an analogue one, unsuited to the online world we have created for ourselves, and in which our children will grow up. Our children, and theirs, will have no qualms about placing their information online, because they will have known no other way.

THE GENERATION GAME

How well did you know your great-grandparents? It's likely that you have very few images of them – perhaps a few stories, or a memento or two handed down to you from your parents. However distant or close you feel to people three generations behind you, your great-grandchildren will have videos, emails, pictures, blogs, social-network pages, audio recordings, digital mementos and physical possessions of you after you have passed on, and many of these items will be archived and fully searchable. In fact, because you are likely to live into your late eighties, assuming that your children (and theirs) have kids in their thirties, you'll meet your great-grandchildren more and more. Your life will be as real to them as those of some of their online 'friends', even after you have passed on.

Digital natives embed their lives in technology. They share the minutiae of their lives through updates with one another using social-networking technology, and share online communication through games.

The children of tomorrow have no choice as to how they will lead these lives online. For them, the internet will have always been there. That's why the notion of privacy we hold will seem restrictive to them. As our children replace us in the workforce, and eventually in positions of power, privacy restrictions will be relaxed gradually, until, by 2050, privacy laws have no real effect on a person's ability to act, interact and react online.

This largely voluntary erosion of privacy will force a choice. Either be online, share and be found, or be offline, and retain privacy. Most people will of course choose a mix of the two choices in different spheres of their lives, as we do now. Today, you might be quite happy to post details of your holiday, or your CV, online. You might be more careful about sharing your sexual preferences. Regardless of your openness in these matters, you would almost certainly want to keep the two parts of your life separate – the professional, and the personal/sexual. Perhaps there will be a split between those who wish to live fully online – where different parts of your online profile are accessible to different communities of which you wish to be a part. Maybe not. Maybe your sexual preferences will form part of your CV, as a means to 'fit' you into a particular organisation, firm or peer group. Either way, prospective employers, partners and friends will have far more information about you than they would have had a mere five years ago. And that is just today. To reiterate: in the future, privacy will be a thing of the past. The task today is to educate our children (and theirs) on the management of information given out and produced online, when everything is online.

DIGITAL LITERACY DEPENDS ON BASIC LITERACY

In an increasingly knowledge-based economy, information is becoming as least as important as land and physical capital. In the future, the distinction between developed and less developed nations won't be the most important at all: distinctions between fast and slow countries, between networked and isolated nations, will dominate[13]. For this reason, the rollout of information and communications technologies is as much a political goal as it is a societal one. We catch up, forge ahead, or fall behind[14], based on the degree to which we pursue the priority of investing in the training of our children in order to deal with the complexity of information which stems from the use of computers and other information and communications technologies. But before we teach them how to surf well, we have to teach them how to read and write, and to express themselves.

Basic literacy skills are vital in enabling children and adults to cope with the challenges they will face in modern Ireland, not least by helping them secure worthwhile employment. For children, inadequate literacy skills create major difficulties[15]. It should come as little surprise, then, that deficiency in basic literacy is greatest among those from disadvantaged areas: almost one-third of children in these areas have severe literacy problems[16]. Nationally, one-tenth of all children face serious literacy difficulties.

There is a continuing failure to tackle the problem. Lack of literacy imposes a significant social and economic cost for the individual and the state. It hinders personal development. The job prospects of those with poor numeracy and literacy skills remain poor, and a high level of illiteracy has a negative impact on broader economic progress. A failure to learn to read or write at primary level means that children are more likely to leave school early, and either find work in low-skilled jobs or become unemployed. Early school-leavers are far more likely to be jobless than those who complete their education. Lack of digital literacy is no different, and, in the coming years, will become worse, as the deepening divide between those who transact online and those who don't deepens the existing inequalities in Irish society.

THE DISTRACTION DISTINCTION: DOES THE INTERNET AFFECT YOUR BRAIN?

In the 1960s, the cultural commentator Marshall McLuhan[17] famously coined the phrase 'the medium is the message'. McLuhan argued that the means by which a piece of information is given to you changes how you perceive it. In short, we are not only *what* we read, but *how* we read[18]. In the future, the effects of online media might become so great as to change how people who constantly use the internet actually think. The concern is that children will not think the way we used to think, that long-term distractibility might end up being worse for them than smoking. The argument is well summarised by *The Atlantic*'s Nicholas Carr[19]:

> I can feel it most strongly when I'm reading. Immersing myself in a book or a lengthy article used to be easy. My mind would get caught up in the narrative or the turns of the argument, and I'd spend hours strolling through long stretches of prose. That's rarely the case any more. Now my concentration often starts to drift after two or three pages. I get fidgety, lose the thread, begin looking for something else to do. I feel as if I'm always dragging my wayward brain back to the text. The deep reading that used to come naturally has become a struggle.

The problem is not just anecdotal. There is evidence that people in high-tech jobs that feature chronic distractability are, in early middle-age, appearing with the same symptoms of burn-out as air-traffic controllers. They might have stress-related diseases, even irreversible brain damage. But the damage is not caused by overwork, but by the distractions that are part of their work. One study found that interruptions take up 2.1 hours of the average knowledge worker's day. The theory is that workers who Google their way through a day, skimming the surface of ideas and events, never learn to develop deep connections between subjects, because their style of reading is so different from that required when reading books. There is no concentration on a topic, only dispersive link-hopping. What emerges from this activity is not a coherent body of knowledge, they suggest, but rather a 'data smog'[20]. There is no consensus on the effects of internet usage on our brains, however: a 2008 study conducted by the Semel Institute for Neuroscience and Human Behavior at UCLA found that middle-aged and older adults who spent time browsing the web every day not only boosted their brain power but could also help prevent cognitive decline such as Alzheimer's disease and dementia later in life.

A host of studies[21] have looked at children's use of information technology, in part to see if it changes how their identities form – whether the way in which children send and receive messages actually alters them as people. Drawing on questionnaires, diaries, semi-structured interviews and focus groups, they found that children who used the internet did so as an extension of their normal, everyday lives, rather than as a replacement for these activities. For example, children would use the internet to work on school problems, interact with friends from school, and so on, rather than creating entirely new identities and experiences for themselves from the (virtual) ground up. So right now, there's not much to worry about.

As I've written, our kids have the curious distinction of being the first generation of digital natives, and many books are now being written to help older generations understand the altered existence their kids have, relative to the experience we (or our parents) had of being teenagers. There are some who think that the state of continuous partial attention (or permanent distraction) brought about by constant exposure to different streams of information from many sources is causing more problems than it might solve.

In 1995, Professor David Meyer's son was killed by a distracted driver who broke a red light[22]. Meyer is a psychologist specialising in attention: how we focus on one thing, rather than another. Attention comes naturally to us; attending to what matters is how we survive and define ourselves. The opposite of attention is distraction – an unnatural condition and one that, as Meyer tragically discovered in 1995, can kill. Meyer is convinced that chronic, long-term distraction is as dangerous as cigarette smoking. In particular, there is the great myth of multitasking. You can't really write an e-mail and speak on the telephone at the same time. Both activities use language, and the language channel in the brain is not built to be used in that way. Multitaskers fool themselves by rapidly switching attention and, as a result, their output deteriorates.

> What information consumes is rather obvious: it consumes the attention of its recipients. Hence, a wealth of information creates a poverty of attention and a need to allocate that attention efficiently among the overabundance of information sources that might consume it.

So writes Herbert Simon, recipient of the Nobel Prize for economics and the A. M. Turing Award, the 'Nobel Prize' of computer science.

This quote defines what I think we need to be teaching our children: methods to deal with a poverty of attention, and tools to manage attention efficiently. In a world where information overload is the norm, those who can navigate through vastly complex architectures of information and data will succeed. Those who can't, or are too far below the basic literacy level even to dream about competing, won't. The choice is really that stark. As far as I am aware (and I've looked), there is no training being given to anyone in Ireland on how to deal with being bombarded by too much information, all the time.

What can we do right now to help our children deal with the type of information-saturated world they might end up living in? Not a lot. Advances in user-interface design will shield much of the information 'noise' users are exposed to. Think of the difference between a Wii console and an old Windows 3.0 operating system. Many of the systems are automated, and simply run in the background until a decision is required. Email and social networks are here to stay. Neither are particularly good at what they are supposed to do – exchange information – but they too will evolve according to the demands of the user. All we can do is try to teach our children how to manage their many 'selves' online, and show them how to be selective with their attention. How we deal with the selection of those selves is the focus of the next chapter.

FACTOID: DIVORCE 3.0: 18 November 2008. Television presenter Debbie Matenopoulos is broken-hearted after learning about her recent divorce from her husband Jay Faires via the Internet. 'I am extremely saddened by the dissolution of my seven-year relationship with my husband,' the host of E!'s *Daily 10* told *People* magazine. 'I am not a proponent of divorce and I believe in working things out,' says Matenopoulos, a two-time Emmy nominee and former co-host of *The View*. 'So you can only imagine my extreme sadness and disillusionment when I was informed of my husband's divorce proceedings, much like you were, by reading them online.'

10 February 2009. A British couple are filing for divorce after the husband's activities in the online world Second Life were brought to light. Lisa Best caught John, or Troy Hammerthall as he is known in Second Life, as he was sat up in bed beside her at 4 AM tapping away on his laptop. Lisa opened an eye and caught sight of the screen. 'I saw John's little person having it off with another man in a dungeon on the screen.'

4

LEISURE SUIT LARRIES

Work just isn't what it used to be.

We do a lot less work than our forebears. From 1820 to 2003, leisure time has increased significantly. One estimate is that labour input per head of population dropped by 47 percent in Japan, 40 percent in the UK, and 23 percent in the US during those years[1]. In short, we have a lot more free time on our hands.

In 1930, the distinguished economist John Maynard Keynes (rhymes with 'brains') wrote *Economic Possibilities for our Grandchildren*. Keynes was concerned with what daily life might be like two generations into the future. He predicted that his grandchildren would be much wealthier than he was – perhaps eight times wealthier. He predicted the emergence of a leisure class of workers, largely freed from the daily grind of work. In 1930, Keynes would have been able to see a significant reduction in the numbers of hours worked.

Between 1870 and 1930, for example, the number of hours worked fell by 30 percent, due to the introduction of labour laws, and increased automation and specialisation. Keynes thought that increased wealth, combined with technological advances like robotics, management science and industrial specialisation, would generate a large surplus of free hours every day, which the average person would use to better themselves – gaining an education, learning an instrument, learning how to paint, and so forth. Keynes forecast that, once the basic needs of life had been catered for, consumption would slow down, and people would be happy with their lots in life. Keynes was wrong about that: we live in a culture of highly conspicuous consumption, where more consumption of everything is always seen as being better than less.

Keynes didn't predict the emergence of television or mass entertainment, nor did he forsee that by 2009, the richer elements of society would be working *more* hours than the poorer elements, not less. There is no 'idle rich' class any more, in the sense that Keynes understood the term. In fact, we now work so much that we get sick when we don't work.

'Leisure sickness' is a condition where seemingly healthy people get sick the second they take a break or go on holiday. The theory goes that, as people start to relax, they begin to listen to signals from their body which ordinarily, while they were active, busy and stressed, they would ignore.

This story plays out with children as well as workers. In the 1980s, researchers wondered whether children's immune systems were being damaged through a lack of exposure to potentially infectious situations in their squeaky-clean homes and schools. Contrasted with the observation that children raised on farms and in rural areas suffered fewer allergic conditions, many children born in urban and suburban areas saw their immune systems react strongly when they were exposed to otherwise harmless allergens. The theory was used to explain the rise in allergic conditions like asthma in developed countries.

The 'overly clean' hypothesis is being replaced by a theory that the real cause of the lack of resistance some children show is a lack of exposure to common microbes. The solution? Dirty up your house, or take a dirt holiday[2], where you'll be exposed to the kind of microbes modern life gets rid of. In effect, you'll be paying to be treated to the kind of holiday your ancestors would have taken for granted as part of their daily lives.

HAMBURGER HEAVEN

In 1891, the first-known hamburger on a bun was served on Grandpa Oscar's farm just west of Tulsa, Oklahoma[3]. Apparently, Grandpa Oscar was the first to add a bun to grated seasoned meat and chopped onions. The chopped-meat recipe was brought over from Germany, and known as the Hamburg steak. Grandpa Oscar's decendents concede that hamburger sandwiches made with bread may predate Grandpa Oscar's famous hamburger, but the total package – toasted bun, chopped meat and onions – all to go, was Grandpa Oscar's, and they claim his place in hamburger heaven for that reason.

The hamburger occupies a strange place in the development of American nutrition. The hamburger is a calorie bomb, designed and built for workers on Oklahoma farms, who worked twelve-hour days rearing cattle, and had time for one, large meal a day – the hamburger[4]. As US society changed from a mainly agricultural one using large amounts of manual labour, to one based primarily on services and sedentary labour practices, its nutrition should have changed, but it didn't. The hamburger is here to stay, and is more popular than ever. Since opening their doors in 1956, McDonalds have made more than 50 billion hamburgers. It might seem trite to say so, but the rise in obesity in developed countries has come largely from the type of food we eat. In today's sedentary world, hamburgers represent a caloric surplus. And where does that caloric surplus go? It shores up around our stomachs, in our arteries, and in our fat cells. Our leisure, paradoxically, has put our health in jeopardy, by helping to make us fat. This is because we didn't, and even now, don't, know how to deal with surpluses.

CALORIC AND COGNITIVE SURPLUSES

Starting after World War II, in the US especially, a whole host of factors, such as growing economic output, rising educational attainment among a new middle class, and increasing life-spans, forced the industrialised world to grapple with something new: truly free time, which is time not devoted to child-rearing or work.

The amount of free time enjoyed by the educated population ballooned. We're talking about billions of hours per year. Most of this newly educated population spent its time watching television. Like industrial change and the hamburger's caloric surplus, increased free time has given us what author Clay Shirky has termed a cognitive surplus.

So, what do we do today with this vast amount of free time? We watch reality TV shows, play video games, talk to our friends and family, 'hang out', do gardening, and a million other very enjoyable pastimes. Some of us 'better ourselves' in the sense that Keynes meant it, by learning an instrument, taking a class, or volunteering our free time to help others. Some of us – in fact, I'd say a lot more of us – don't. We just sit there, eating and watching someone get voted off. This is a feature of every modern society. Let's take Canada, for example. In 2008, Canadians watched television for an average of twenty-five hours a week. Twenty percent of them spend at least forty hours in front of a screen. Multiplied by the adult (sixteen years or more) population of Canada (28.1 million people), that 20 percent which watches forty hours or more – that's 5.6 million people – spends 225 *million* hours watching television each week, or 117 *billion* hours per year. And that's just that 20 percent of Canada's population.

Let's repeat that simple calculation for Ireland's adult population: we have around 3.26 million people over sixteen. If 20 percent of them watch at least forty hours or more of TV a week, then we have 1.3 billion hours being spent per year just watching, well, TV. In the USA, *200 billion* hours per year are spent watching television. And TV is now the equivalent of a half-time job for many people in Ireland.

Isn't that scary?

Now, though, for the first time in its history, younger people are watching less TV than their elders. The cause of the decline is competition for their free time from media that allow for active and social participation, not just passive and individual consumption. The value of media is no longer in sources but in *flows*; when we pool our cognitive surplus, it creates value that doesn't exist when we operate in isolation. The displacement of TV watching is coming among people who are using some of their time to make things and do things, sometimes alone and sometimes together, and to share these things with others. Wikipedia is the best and most obvious example: an individually authored but collaboratively curated knowledge engine.

Shirky has calculated that even if 1 percent of the people in the US stopped watching TV, they could build nearly a hundred Wikipedias every year with their free time.

Shirky[5] believes that 'we can take advantage of our cognitive surplus, but only if we start regarding pure consumption as an anomaly, and broad participation as the norm. This is not a dispassionate argument, because the stakes are so high. We don't get to decide whether we want a new society. The changes we are experiencing can't be rolled back, nor contained in the present institutional frameworks. What we might get to decide is how we want this change to turn out.'

BUT JUST HOW DO WE DECIDE? THE PARADOX OF CHOICE

In 2004, psychologist Barry Schwartz went to a shop to buy some pants. He wanted jeans. The last time he bought jeans, they came in one style: 501s with a straight leg. Schwartz left the shop after several hours, completely upset by what he had experienced. Jeans don't come in one shape with one colour and one waist any more: there are hundreds, if not thousands, of choices to make to get the perfect pair of jeans for you. Schwartz was overwhelmed by what he came to call 'the paradox of choice'[6]. The paradox is that, in the presence of a virtually infinite number of contrasting alternatives, you are almost certainly going to run out of time, energy or money before you get the perfect combination for you, even for a simple purchase like jeans. The abundance of choice, paradoxically, often leads to depression and feelings of loneliness: foreknowledge of your inevitable failure to choose the right one directly affects your happiness. Schwartz writes:

Autonomy and freedom of choice are critical to our well-being, and choice is critical to freedom and autonomy. Nonetheless, though modern Americans have more choice than any group of people ever has [*sic*] before, and thus, presumably, more freedom and autonomy, we don't seem to be benefiting from it psychologically.

What has the paradox of choice got to do with our cognitive surplus? Well, with increasing numbers of things to do, see and make online, the only really scarce resource is your attention. And the web is, for all practical purposes, nearly infinite. Most work in the twenty-first century will be knowledge work – moving digital things around to create new digital things. Given a completely blank and practically infinite canvas, how do you decide what to make, see or do?

Most people use simple rules, look at what everyone else is doing, and rely on habit, to avoid making stressful choices. Schwartz provides simple rules for figuring out choices. Ask: what do you want? The goal you're trying to achieve will be crucial in deciding the path you need to take to get to that goal. Ask: how important is this goal? Array the options you have available. Perhaps the goal is unattainable, perhaps not. Pick the winning option, and go for it. If you don't reach your goal, figure out why not, and perhaps change your goal.

These coping skills for dealing with complexity of choice in the twenty-first century are not being taught to our children, because the tools scarcely exist at the moment. It's up to us to make these tools available, and soon. From the truly mundane problem of buying jeans, to the more profound challenges of balancing career, family, and our individual needs, the range of choices we have has become part of the problem, not the solution, because our obsession with choice encourages us to seek that which makes us feel worse.

In the next chapter, we will see that information overload

and paradoxical choices might be the least of our problems in 2050, with changes in the climate and our ecosystem affecting the quality of life of every person in Ireland in the next forty years.

CAR TROUBLE

10 April 2050

Jack Murphy's car needs to be replaced. The car's battery won't charge beyond 40 percent, the bodywork is looking a little dated, and there's a baby coming. Also, because the flooding on their morning commute is getting worse, Jack is thinking that a larger, more all-terrain vehicle with a big boot would be better. Thanks to a host of environmental taxes levied on larger cars, the cost of the car is going to hit Jack right in the wallet, and just as his business is cash-strapped.

Jack is not impressed. The dealer is nice enough, offering to take the older car and break it down for Jack, completing the life cycle of the car from design to production to use to destruction and finally to reuse.

In fact, the dealer offers Jack a discount if he agrees to use some of the old car in the construction of the new fabricated object that will eventually become his Granddad-mobile, as Maeve is calling it. Jack bargains the dealer down a bit, and gets him to agree to print a new pram out of part of the old car as well, for the baby. The dealer agrees, and hangs up the call to check the specs of the new pram.

Maeve is beginning to show a little, and her morning sickness is the talk of the house. Maeve's school have been informed of her pregnancy, and are taking steps to alter her coursework to fit in with the new arrival. Maeve will take the autumn off, and do her Leaving Certificate in the next September. Maeve's sometime boyfriend, Patrick, is nowhere to be seen, and the uncertainty of their relationship is worrying Maeve and driving down her test scores and affecting her project work. Sarah is worried about Maeve, and thinks about her a lot at work. Sarah often tunes into Maeve's life feed to see what she's up to when there is a spare second at the hospital. Maeve tells her not to worry. Sarah worries anyway.

The dealer calls Jack back. The car will be printed in about a week. All Jack must do is arrange finance, choose the interior of the car, and the colour of the pram. Jack finishes the call with the dealer, sits at his desk drinking coffee, and thinks about colours for cars, colours for prams, and cash flow for someday cash cows.

5

THE ENVIRONMENT OF IRELAND IN 2050: HOT, FLAT AND CROWDED

Ireland in 2050 will feel like a much smaller place. There may be more than 7 million people alive in Ireland by 2050 – a figure not seen on this island since the 1840s[1]. The effects of a larger, longer-lived population will be dramatic, but these demographic effects are only part of the story. While population growth on its own will cause population densities across the country to increase dramatically[2], the effects of climate change, which are the subject of this chapter, will cause a further shrinkage of the island we live on due to coastal erosion, flooding, and water shortages. Thanks to climate change, Ireland will be a different place, and the Irish people will be subtly different, too.

One in ten people will be over eighty years of age in 2050[3], and one in four will be over sixty-five. Compare this to today, where we have only one in twelve people in Ireland over sixty-five. Chapter 7 will discuss the effects of an increased population on Irish society, culture and economy, but here, let's take it as read that there will be more people in Ireland, and that more of them (that's you and me) will be older. An older population will change Irish culture and community, as well as having an impact on our health service. We'll explore these issues in later chapters. For now, let's say that our island will be more crowded, with more people, many of whom will be older, and this will affect the environment. The environment we live in will change, and we will change with it. But what will happen to your locality? Do the experts have an answer to the question: how will climate change affect me?

Let's talk about climate change itself. Climate change centres on the issue of greenhouse-gas proliferation. But what does that mean? Concentrated human economic activities like agriculture and industry produce carbon dioxide, nitrous oxide, and methane, as well as other harmful gases. These gases increase the amount of sunlight the planet absorbs through its atmosphere, so the temperature of the planet increases. This effect, known as global warming, has been observed since the 1800s following the Industrial Revolution, and the existence of global warming is now a matter of agreed-upon and established scientific fact.

The effects of climate change on Ireland have been studied intensively by Professor John Sweeney of NUI, Maynooth, and his colleagues at the Irish Climate Analysis and Research Units – ICARUS[4].

ICARUS is a research outfit which produces local estimates of a global climate model developed by international researchers[5]. Its purpose is to ask what the likely effects of climate change will be on the island of Ireland. Their work could not be more relevant, timely or important, and they are not alone. Several government agencies[6] and other research units[7] around the country, and many around the world, are working to understand the likely effects of climate change on Ireland and the world as a whole. ICARUS reports that 1998 was the warmest year of the warmest decade of the warmest century in at least the last millennium. Climate change is happening to the planet, and it will continue to happen to the world of our grandchildren living in Ireland in 2050. For them, global warming and climate change will be less of an academic question, and more of a reality. Their grandchildren, in 2100, will experience the full effects of global warming, but in 2050 the likely path of the planet's reaction will be known with more certainty.

Before we discuss the impact of climate change on Ireland in 2050, let's ask: how do the boffins at ICARUS make their predictions, and how much store should we set by them?

ICARUS builds and interprets the outputs of a model of the Irish climate under different scenarios: good, bad and indifferent. But what does that mean? A model is basically a story and, using the real world as the basis for the story, the model creates different endings for the story, called scenarios. The story of what is happening to our climate is like the plot of Disney's *Snow White*. Imagine that you've never read *Snow White* or seen the film, and you start reading. Now, let's say that the point in the story where Snow White gets lost in the forest after being turfed out of the palace by the evil queen is today.

We can see that things are not looking good for Snow White, but because we have not read the story through to the end, we don't yet know how good or bad things might actually get for her. If you were to stop the story there, not knowing for sure what might happen to her, and ask yourself

93

what the likely outcomes Snow White might face are, you might generate a range of different endings for the story, or scenarios, for her.

Maybe Snow White walks out of the forest and is never heard from again. Maybe she dies in the forest. Maybe she finds a small house and decides to live in the forest. Maybe something unexpected happens. You don't know for certain. But you are sure that her options, sitting in the forest, terrified and alone, range between untimely death and happily ever after. You probably won't predict the appearance of the dwarves (unless you've read the full title of the story), but most likely, Snow White has a hard time, and then things get a bit better for her.

Now compare the ending you have come up with as the most likely – she has a hard time but things mostly work out – to the ending you know takes place in the story. Snow White meets some dwarves (didn't see that coming). Snow White eats a poisoned apple (OK, things got worse for her), and she is rescued by the Prince and they live happily ever after (OK, things get better).

It's easy to see that your scenario missed some of the details of the story, but crucially, the scenario caught the story's broad strokes. We can change the endings of the story to make them better, or worse, and to generate different scenarios as we see fit: Snow White dead in the forest, Snow White becoming queen following a coup d'état, whatever.

What matters for us when writing alternative endings to the climate-change story for Ireland is the broad strokes, but applied as locally as possible.

The predictions of the ICARUS team are like the different paths in the Snow White story. Starting from today, they look back at how the climate has been changing, using evidence gathered by geographers, climatologists and geologists, about the environment. That process takes them to the point in the forest – they have a good knowledge of the past and present, and this knowledge is continually getting better as more data is gathered and analysed. Then they generate a range of 'worst case', 'best case', and 'middling case' scenarios to ask themselves what the effects might be on Ireland's climate.

The stories (or models) developed and maintained by ICARUS break the map of Ireland up into squares. Imagine taking a map of the island of Ireland and, using a pen and ruler, doing just that. Make a hundred squares, on a ten-by-ten grid. Some of the squares fall on coastal areas like Dublin, Galway and Cork. Other squares are almost completely landlocked, like the area around Kilkenny. Some are over mountains and rivers. Some squares are just city sprawl.

The model asks: what will happen to the areas in these squares, given what we know about the geography, geology and other factors inside that square. Will we see more flooding in that square, or less? Will temperatures increase, and if so, by how much? The question of locality only matters when the size of the square gets small enough.

Right now, the squares in the model are about 200 kilometres across. This is too large to make accurate predictions about your town or your property in most cases, but for the local area of which you are a part, the model fares well. ICARUS and its researchers have 'downscaled' the larger model to regional levels, however, and while their findings for the lives of the middle class in 2050 make for heavy reading, it is better to know and to adapt in the presence of that knowledge. As research progresses, the degree of precision of the scientists' estimates will only increase.

How accurate are the predictions of the scientists' model? No model is entirely accurate or correct, but if the model is a good one, it gets the story right in broad strokes.

One way we can test the efficacy of this model is to ask it to predict something we already know: the past. Start the model from 1985, say, and, based on information from the past, before 1985, ask the model to predict what will happen from 1985 to 2000. Then check the predictions of the model's scenarios against the data we know for sure. We then have a good measure of the model's accuracy. The model developed by ICARUS predicts changes in temperature, water usage and rainfall quite accurately. We can believe what the climate scientists are telling us. Once we believe what the models tell us, however, we have to do something about the predictions thrown up by the model.

So, finally, what's going to happen to Ireland's environment by 2050?

The ICARUS team report that, by 2050, January mean temperatures will increase by 1.5 degrees Celsius[8], and we will see summer temperatures going up by 2.5 degrees. This prediction is based on their 'medium' scenario, where, as in the Snow White example, things get bad initially and then better at the end. (So we'll have milder winters, and warmer summers. If you're smiling reading this line and thanking God for deliverance from awful summers, don't. This is not a good thing.)

This increase in temperature means that Ireland will have long, hot summers, averaging 25 degrees in the summer months, and milder, wetter winters, with winter rainfall expected to jump by 10 percent for the entire country. Not all regions will experience this change equally over the year. Areas like the north-west of Ireland will see their winter rainfall go up by 20 percent, while the south-west will see its rainfall decrease by 40 percent in the summer months. This change in rainfall patterns will have consequences for agriculture. Our current crop and livestock production will be increasingly challenged. Agriculture is considered one of the sectors most adaptable to changes in climate. However, increased heat, pests, water stress, diseases, and weather extremes will pose adaptation challenges for crop and livestock production.

The uneven distribution of rainfall in Ireland in 2050 means that the irrigation of crops and land will become a priority long before our grandchildren have to worry about climate change. Irrigation is costly, and only makes sense economically if the water used for irrigation, which will be in short supply in 2050, is free. Water charges will come at some point in the next forty years, making maintaining current agricultural outputs very difficult, as the farmers will not be able to make a profit[9].

Sensible, profit-minded farmers will reduce their irrigation needs by adapting their land to produce other, more tolerant crops. So Ireland of the green fields, with its traditional emphasis on livestock, may become a thing of the past by 2050. The crops our new climate will grow best will be soybean, barley, maize and other types of wheat, which are hardier and do better in this new climate, with its more limited access to water in the summers.

Which countries currently experience weather like Ireland in 2050, with mild, wet winters and warm, dry summers? Places like Algeria now have wet winters, with a January temperature of 9 degrees, and winter rainfalls comparable to those of Ireland in 2050. Summers in Algeria average 26 degrees in July, with very little rainfall – similar to what we are likely to see in the south of Ireland in 2050. The crops they grow in Algeria are wheat, barley, oats and grapes[10]. There is a model of how people live and grow crops in these temperatures and with this climate: Algerians are living with this climate as I write this. The challenge for Ireland in the medium term is to adapt in as efficient a manner as possible, while attempting to maintain as much of what makes us Irish as possible.

I wrote at the start of the chapter that Ireland would be a smaller place, but how much smaller? For every 1 centimetre rise in sea level caused by Arctic ice melting, our coastline will be eroded by 1 metre. So, if the climate-change models are correct, Ireland in 2050 will lose 300 square kilometres of land as the sea encroaches. We would lose an area about the size of the Burren by 2050. Areas like Louth, Waterford and north Dublin are under threat in this scenario, but cities near rivers like Galway and Limerick will experience more seasonal flooding as well.

So coastal flooding increases, and the ground water we use for drinking may become tainted with salt water, meaning that our access to clean, clear water will be further reduced unless we put desalination and anti-flooding measures in place where it is cost-effective to do so. We will have to abandon some of the land entirely. Ireland will be a smaller place.

Changing temperatures, weather fluctuations, economic development and its resultant pollution have combined to reduce the range of Ireland's natural flora and fauna, while introducing other, more exotic, plants and animals. Our biodiversity is changing. Relatively, Ireland's biodiversity is not that high – about nine hundred plants are indigenous. Compared to the biodiversity of the Amazon, this is nothing, but still, our plants and animals make up a large part of our environment. Losing too many of the indigenous species which make Ireland what it is would diminish us. There are, however, preventative regulations in place which will only be strengthened over time. Places like the Burren could be threatened by flooding and increased temperatures, but really these areas contain most of the biodiversity, and funding exists to help maintain these areas pretty well already. Increasing the protection we afford these areas should go some way towards reducing the impact our development has had, and will continue to have, on our island's biodiversity. The question is: will this protection come too late to save a significant number of species from disappearing?

The next challenge facing Ireland in 2050 is the risk of floods and storms. The increased rainfall caused by climate change will be accompanied by storms and flash floods, like those we saw in August 2008, when the M50 was closed because a section of it was underwater. On the night of 9 August, a record 76.2 mm of rain fell, overwhelming sewage and drainage systems, which were already strained due to a high tide. Large sections of the infrastructure around Dublin were closed for twenty-four hours while the water was pumped off, businesses in Kildare and Celbridge had the contents of their stores destroyed by flooding, and a train derailed. Also, homes across Ireland were damaged; many were uninsured for flooding because of the rarity of the event. Lives were lost on the roads due to the perilous driving conditions experienced during those days.

The record 76.2 mm of rainfall broke the previous national record set in 1986 by Hurricane Charlie. In Cork, the rainfall record was set in 1975, and that too was broken[11].

The flash flooding we saw in August 2008 is a once-in-a-century, rare-as-owl's-teeth event. The trouble is that, thanks to climate change, we will see more of these 'freak' occurrences, and their impacts will only worsen. A once-in-a-century event will become a once-in-a-decade event. This is a cause for concern.

The good news is that we have adapted already. Ordinary

people are taking out flood insurance for their homes and businesses. Plans are being drawn up to change the drainage systems on major Irish roads like the M50. The county councils are working on flood defences of rivers whose banks might swell and overrun in a very bad storm, in order to minimise the damage caused. But it's not all good news, as it is difficult to plan for these events because of their rarity.

Rare events are, by definition, unlikely, and don't show up often enough in the past to make us take account of them when we are looking to the future. Think about the 9/11 terrorist attacks[12]. These were highly unlikely events, and largely unpredicted by the majority of the population. To most people, they were 'black swan' events[13]: highly important, but very rare, and practically unpredictable. Black swan events can be personal – like having a car crash or developing cancer – or they can be much larger – for example, the stock market crash of 1929, which almost no one forsaw. The consequences of that event are still being felt today.

When we think about making our homes, businesses and infrastructure safe against flash floods and freak occurrences, there will always be the tendency to seek the average when costing the measures to prevent these events. Like Snow White and her seven scenarios, it is tempting to take the average outcome, where things aren't too rosy, but not too bad either. If you take the average scenario as most likely (and why wouldn't you?) and an extreme event occurs, then you will not be prepared to handle that extreme event.

A general lesson is: if an event, like the rainfall we saw in August 2008, is rare and extreme, meaning that it is unlikely that you have seen something this bad before, and your defence against that is only average, then you will experience problems.

Drainage systems around the country were overwhelmed

by the flooding, because they did not have the capacity to cope with an extreme event. The sewage and drainage systems on Irish roads were not designed to deal with 76.2 mm of rainfall in one twenty-four-hour period. Homes which were close to rivers whose banks had not burst in living memory were flooded – to the shock of the home-owners.

The influence of extreme weather events on Irish life will only increase for our grandchildren in 2050. How they cope with these events will be determined largely by the planning processes we put in place to ensure that the impacts of these rare events are reduced for the average Irish person. People and institutions are already adapting. It is just a question of how much to adapt.

Despite increased rainfall in the south, Ireland in 2050 will suffer occasional droughts during the drier summer months, especially in Dublin and its environs[14] as well as Athlone, Cork, and Galway. The issue facing the Irish water supply is simple supply and demand. Right now, the system just about allows us to think that water is an unlimited resource. That will change in the next five to ten years.

We have a water budget every year, comprised of the rainfall we experience, the saturation level of the soil, the amount of water lost to evaporation, and runoff[15].

The water we all receive is filtered through rivers, lakes and reservoirs, then travels through cleaning stations, through taps and pipes, to our homes, businesses and farms.

The demand for water in Ireland today is around 500 million litres a day, with a population of 4.1 million[16]. With the population expected to increase to 7 million people by 2050, the demand for water will only increase. Businesses need it to run their industrial processes. (This demand will decrease on average over the next forty years as the composition of Irish business changes, but in absolute terms the demand for water from business will almost certainly be greater.) Houses need water for obvious reasons.

Researchers have calculated that, in total, when you look at the production process from start to end, it takes 11,000 litres of water to make a cheeseburger, and 83,000 litres of water to make a medium-sized family car, especially when you add in the cost of industrial production[17]. The average person uses 135 litres of water every day, and most of this is wasted. Water – or more precisely the lack of it – will be everywhere in the future. It might seem like a paradox, but scarcity will abound.

The scarcity of H_2O is being caused by growing populations in countries like India and China, but it's also being caused by consumerism and development in regions like North America and Europe. Urbanisation and climate change are also major factors, and in many cases the problem won't be a lack of water per se, but water in the wrong places.

In China, some areas are already taking legal action against other regions whom they accuse of stealing 'their' rain through cloud seeding, while in other countries the problem is too much rain rather than not enough. The pollution of rivers and lakes will move to centre stage politically in Ireland and abroad, local dams will become global issues, and people's attitudes and behaviour towards water will change significantly. Every industry, from agriculture to fashion, will come into the spotlight with regard to water use in Ireland, and customers will select one product or brand over another based on the company's water policy as much as on any other aspect of their branding and cost bases.

With a dry season and a larger population forecast for 2050, Ireland will experience water shortages in areas like Dublin as early as 2015. How?

The simple answer is that Dublin's rapid growth over the

last fifteen years has not seen a corresponding growth in the infrastructure necessary to support these new economic activities properly. The result is a looming water shortage, with local councils considering tapping the Shannon basin to feed Dublin's growing need for water. This measure would certainly affect local pollution levels and local tourism and biodiversity, but it may be the only real option available to policymakers in 2015.

The other option to increase the supply of clean water would be a desalination plant in north Dublin, by the bay. Desalination plants are extremely costly to set up, run and maintain, so the price of water will have to rise from its current level of zero for households, to something which forces consumers to think about the amounts of water they are using from day to day and to decide on how much of that water they actually need to use.

The fact that one can go on a two-week holiday and leave a tap running, and return with no consequences, is a testament to the level of inefficiency in the system of water production in Ireland.

So, expect a water rate for households to come in sometime between 2015 and 2020 and to rise steadily above the rate of inflation for the foreseeable future as water becomes a relatively scarce resource.

This change will come in waves. First, policymakers will try the desalination route, because it is less politically damaging to build a large, job-creating water-cleansing plant than to tax 2 million households, all of whom contain voters. But as the population of Dublin – and Ireland as a whole – increases beyond the ability of policymakers to stop the demand for water from outstripping supply, eventually either the Shannon will have to be tapped to provide more drinking water for Dublin at the expense of tourism and pollution levels in Munster, or a general water rate will be introduced. As the cost of water increases, so this water rate will increase also. Don't forget that service provision will increase over time as well, so the services that households, businesses and farms receive will become more efficient. But don't expect this increase in efficiency to cope with a near-doubling of the population in fifty years.

Irish daily life will not be much affected by these changes. Watering summer lawns will be a rich person's pastime, but the basic necessities of water delivery, waste disposal, and industrial and agricultural needs will be met, most likely at an increased amount per person than today. There will be no free-for-all with regard to water provision, as there is now.

HOW WILL A CHANGING ENVIRONMENT AFFECT THE AVERAGE MIDDLE-CLASS FAMILY IN 2050?

First, they will pay for their water usage, and this will affect their behaviour. For example, few families will have large stretches of manicured leafy grass: in the dry season, it will die. Expect to see hardier grass substitutes being used. Farms will begin changing their planting practices to accommodate a wetter, warmer winter and a drier, warmer summer. Ireland's traditional staples of livestock and dry-stock farming will change, and be replaced by crops which can make the most of our changing climate, like soybean, rapeseed and wheat (plants which, as we have seen, thrive in places like Algeria). Typical temperatures in Ireland in the summer months (22 to 28 degrees in July and August) will be quite pleasant for everyone who is not a farmer, and will in fact make Ireland a tourist destination for people who want either some sunshine, or a little less.

As the world warms up, people will begin looking to go to places where they can avoid the summer heat, rather than travel to it. So Ireland's weather, which counts as a negative in international sun tourism, might change for the better and make us a popular destination for people wishing to escape other, hotter climes.

Our middle-class family will have to contend with more floods and inundations if they live near a river or close to the sea. Here, the important point to remember is that these floods will not happen every winter, or every summer, but our family will experience a very bad storm, say, once every ten years.

The increased frequency of rare and damaging environmental events will be a feature of modern Irish life in 2050. Insurance premia, the housing stock and people's behaviour will all adapt accordingly. For example, if a family wishes to locate near a river, significantly higher insurance premia may force them to make other living-arrangement choices, especially if the house (and the family) is older. Remember, the houses constructed during the housing boom of 2002–08 will be forty years old at this stage, and probably in need of repair, renovation or demolition, so if they are close to rivers or in areas like north Dublin – which will experience regular flooding – they might be abandoned or demolished altogether as uninhabitable.

The weather will not, by and large, change living patterns for the average Irish family by 2050. By 2070 and 2100, the full effects of climate change will be felt, so your grandchildren and their children will experience the consequences of your decisions today, and those of your parents yesterday. In 2050, the consequences of increased erosion, flooding, and water shortages for a larger population that is more dependent than ever on water reserves will simply cause a reduction in the number of choices the average family will have when they are considering where to live.

As we will see in a later chapter, because of the political choices Irish people have made in the past, and most likely will continue to make in the future, inequality between classes of people resident in Ireland will mean that there will be fewer choices for the poor as to where to live: the price of land – and the price of property built on that land – will be out of their reach, and the government will be expected to take up the slack over time, providing residential housing (of an inferior quality). This inequality will breed near-ghettos in areas that are close to environmentally compromised regions, and the poor will suffer (as they always have), increasing the level of inequality in the economy still further.

DUBLIN AS A NEW LOS ANGELES

In 2050, Dublin will be the size Los Angeles is now, with a corresponding population density and similar average living standards. Locating the family in certain areas within the Dublin-Kildare-Meath-Wicklow-Wexford conurbation will be undesirable because of increased risks of flooding. The family's insurance premia, and the price of the house itself, will reflect that fact, and the family will make its decision on whether to live in this area or not based partly on these factors. Today, risk insurance is a fairly trivial matter when one thinks about buying a house. Not so in 2050, when widespread flooding will cause insurance premia to rise dramatically as the effects of climate change become more apparent.

Another factor which might change the average middle-class family's mind when locating in a particular area is the number of people living in that area, and the air pollution associated with it. Places like south County Dublin, from O'Connell Street to Greystones, will essentially be large mixtures of housing, light industry, services, housing, and more housing. Expect to see the ban on constructing buildings that are thirty-plus storeys high disappear in the early 2020s as population densities in Dublin close in on Dutch and US averages, making it cost-effective and profitable to build large apartment blocks that are integrated with shopping facilities.

The housing stock will change as well. I have already mentioned that once large, integrated apartment blocks become more economically viable, they will become a feature of modern Irish life. I haven't said anything about the *sustainability* of these houses.

By 2050, planning regulations will have adapted to cope with the effects of climate change on Irish life by mandating certain strictures in the size and material composition of the house, as well as its location. Technology in housing will advance to meet the demands of a more ecologically aware consumer and provider, but as long as concrete and steel are the cheapest products on the market, businesses will seek them out. Regulating better insulation, glass and materials is a large part of what a sensible county planning office should do, and with increased pressure on land, for the reasons I've outlined above, it will make sense to insist on these regulations at source rather than waiting for business to generate them through increased adoption of better technology.

If the family wishes to locate in a rural area, it should expect to pay for the privilege. Land, which is becoming cheaper as the property bubble subsides, will become expensive in 2050 as people's desire for relative solitude goes up in step with a rising population. In any case, the family will see these constraints, and make their decisions about location accordingly. It is important to stress that normal life will go on, in spite of the effects of climate change. What might change is the definition of 'normal': who would have thought of coming to Ireland for a sun tan?

FLOOD WARNING

11 April 2050

It's springtime. Jack needs to sort out Maeve's birthing plan if she needs to go to a local clinic. There might be complications. Jack is finding it hard to keep his cool about the new baby. Maeve is starting to show. She is four months along now. Spring floods are not affecting their home because of its elevation, but the smaller roads on the way into Dublin, which are not reinforced by the local council, do flood, and Jack is thinking in terms of end-of-the-world type disaster scenarios today. This is not helped by Maeve changing her phone's avatar to a picture of the baby *in utero*, which comes up on his screen whenever she calls or messages. Seeing an unborn baby every time you get a call can be slightly unnerving.

Jack doesn't know what to say to Maeve. Their talk in early March did not go well. She stormed off angrily before he got a chance to say what he wanted. What he wanted to say was 'look, I went through this myself, in a way, and I think you'll do fine. Whatever happens, I'm here for you'. What Jack actually said while standing over her with his hands on his hips like a superhero was: 'Look here, any chance that boyfriend of yours is going to show up again? Because if not, that's OK with us, really'. Maeve looked at Jack like he had three heads, then got upset and ran off. Jack told his wife Sarah what he said, and Sarah wasn't exactly thrilled with Jack's performance. Jack thanked a higher power when a call came through for him announcing a crisis with Jack's Chinese suppliers. If the call hadn't come through, Jack would have had to invent a ninja attack or something. So, rather than deal with Maeve right now, Jack is planning for disaster scenarios around Maeve, worrying if there will be enough sunblock stocked to avoid the usual summer heatwave, and scanning the horizon for ninjas.

6

POWERING A POST-INDUSTRIAL IRELAND

Energy is the master resource, because energy enables us to convert one material into another. As natural scientists continue to learn more about the transformation of materials from one form to another with the aid of energy, energy will be even more important . . . For example, low energy costs would enable people to create enormous quantities of useful land. The cost of energy is the prime reason that water desalination now is too expensive for general use; reduction in energy cost would make water desalination feasible, and irrigated farming would follow in many areas that are now deserts. And if energy were much cheaper, it would be feasible to transport sweet water from areas of surplus to arid areas far away. Another example: if energy costs were low enough, all kinds of raw materials could be mined from the sea.

JULIAN SIMON[1]

Anyone who thinks that wind and solar power will replace coal- and oil-powered electricity generation in the short term just hasn't done their sums. Each renewable energy source is either too scarce or too unreliable to replace coal, oil and gas. It's worthwhile remembering why fossil fuels powered the Industrial Revolutions which brought increased living standards to billions of people, generation after generation. Fossil fuels are concentrated, plentiful, storable and, perhaps most importantly for Ireland, *transportable* sources of energy. Just for contrast, today's wind farms need a five hundred-tonne concrete base support and four thousand windmills to equal the output of one coal-burning station, and the energy wind farms provide is not reliable, because it's driven by the wind. The maths just do not add up. Not yet.

This chapter argues that Ireland needs to embrace a nuclear future in the medium term, until renewable energy can take up the increased demand for electricity our post-industrial society will have by 2050. The argument I'll present here is not for nuclear power as the be-all and end-all of energy production, but rather as a necessary evil that must be endured to secure the economy's development until a transition to renewable power generation technologies can be achieved.

A NUCLEAR IRELAND?

As an island, Ireland imports the vast majority of its energy in the form of fossil fuels like coal and oil, and, increasingly, gas. Given the reality of climate change and the coming of what is called 'Peak Oil' – where the production of oil becomes ever more costly as the likelihood of finding more oil decreases – the need for a growing economy to provide itself with power without burning fossil fuels is becoming ever more pressing[2]. Even when taken together, solar, wind, wave, hydroelectric and other greener technologies are not yet up to the task of supplying Ireland's needs, as the Irish government's 2007 white paper on the subject has shown. The migration to alternative, renewable energy sources will take a significant amount of time to plan and implement. Due to the depletion of fossil-fuel resources worldwide, we don't have enough conventional energy sources to support the building of this infrastructure if we assume continuing growth and 'business as usual' for this period of time. The expense of the anticipated infrastructure will place an almost unendurable strain on the economy if we try to make the conversion too quickly. The lag time required to switch our economies over to renewable energy sources is just too long.

Environmental campaigner and scientist Dr James Lovelock, originator of the Gaia theory of the Earth's ecology as a forced-feedback system, has controversially written that, in the short to medium term – say twenty-five years or so – nuclear power is the only option for advanced economies to grow without fossil fuels. After that, I believe that each of these technologies will, of necessity, form the backbone of our power-generation needs. But until then, a substitute for ever-more-expensive fossil fuels needs to be found in order to allow the Irish economy to grow. That substitute is nuclear power.

Ireland has repeatedly rejected the construction of a nuclear power plant for a host of reasons, most of them irrational, factually incorrect, or just twaddle. Critics of nuclear power point to the costs of nuclear power being, in this order, high-level waste disposal, risk of proliferation, threat of severe accidents, and risk of terrorism. Obviously, Ireland would not be subject to most of these risks as it is a (largely) neutral country. I think that if the benefits of nuclear power were put to the Irish people in a consistent and intelligent way, they would respond with a different answer.

FACTOID: Nuclear produces no pollution, has a sound safety record, and compares with oil on cost, although some commentators, such as environmentalist Amory Lovins, claim that nuclear power is too expensive to produce when we factor in its safety record. Seventy percent of Americans now favour the nuclear option, and 88 percent of those living near nuclear plants are confident about their safety. New designs, like the pebble-bed reactor, are immune from meltdown and store waste in glass safely for 200,000 years. A 'fast breeder' design recycles spent fuel to reduce radioactive waste from 95 percent to 1 percent of the fuel used, increasing efficiency and reducing the size of the disposal problem. One approach, based on thorium instead of uranium, uses up dangerous weapons-grade plutonium and produces half as much radioactive waste as uranium-based options, and the waste is active for only a hundred years compared with the thousands of years current radioactive waste remains harmful for. Other possible designs include the sodium-cooled fast reactor and the high-temperature reactor.

The benefit of nuclear power is the creation of cheap, reliable energy, which is independent of fossil-fuel usage and price changes. Not only does nuclear power have negligible CO_2 emissions (which lead to global warming), but nuclear power produced in the Western Hemisphere has never killed a member of the public or had any measurable impact on public health – miles of column inches to the contrary. France is the shining example of the benefits of nuclear power: 78 percent of French electricity is generated using nuclear fuel, there have been no nuclear-power-related accidents in the country's history, and there are plans to build more nuclear plants in the coming years in both France and the United Kingdom. The worst disaster in nuclear power generation – Chernobyl – is now a nature reserve in all but name. The exclusion zone around the Chernobyl nuclear power station is teeming with wildlife[3], because humans have left the area untouched for a long period of time.

Running out of uranium isn't really an issue either, at least until 2050: there are approximately 14,750,000 tonnes of the stuff on Earth. Last year we used close to 67,000 tonnes of uranium. Japanese researchers are currently considering the possibility of constructing giant undersea sponge farms to collect uranium suspended in seawater. Namibia, in particular, has the potential to become another Saudi Arabia. Namibia's deserts contain uranium deposits, which have not been exploited until now. With types four (and five) fast breeder reactor technologies, we would have practically unlimited energy resources into the twenty-second century – safer, cleaner, and cheaper than fossil fuels.

The main containment vessel for nuclear waste is concrete. Already, ultra-high-density concrete technologies are being developed, meaning that a containment vessel for nuclear waste built to last 100 years with today's concrete could last up to 16,000 years if made with an ultra-high-density concrete. The problems of nuclear energy production are being solved, as increased demand for nuclear power stations enables a renaissance in research in the area.

It should be remembered that Ireland is contributing to climate change in much the same way as India and China, albeit on a much smaller scale. Right now, our CO_2 emissions are 24 percent higher than the 1990 levels. Our Kyoto protocol agreement is for 13 percent increases in CO_2 emissions. Ireland's energy needs are set to increase by 25 percent by 2015 alone. It is not unreasonable to assume a further doubling of demand for electricity from 2015 to 2050, given a developing economy and a larger population. If our power needs will only ever increase in the next forty-one years, then energy provision is not a problem which will go away. Security of energy sources is a strategic imperative for Ireland, as security is the key to continued economic growth. Without cheap power, the economy will wither.

Our policymakers do not see it this way, however, or at the most pay lip service to the notion of a long-term energy strategy for Ireland.

No nation can grow, and increase its general standard of living, without plentiful sources of energy. Political and economic stability are predicated on cheap energy. Continually increasing economic growth driven by an increasing population that has an expectation of improving standards of living demands a continuing increase in energy production using natural resources.

You see this problem most clearly in developing countries. Developing nations need reliable, efficient, cost-effective energy to bring households out of poverty, to install and strengthen democracy, develop a middle class, grow commerce, and produce higher-value goods and services to enrich both its citizens and itself through world trade. Ireland, as a newly developed nation, has the ability to buy in its energy needs from abroad, and can grow its economy at the same time, as long as the price of energy is low enough. World energy markets are, to say the least, turbulent. The more energy we produce at home, the more insulated we are from this turbulence. The problem is that Ireland's greatest natural renewable resources – wind and hydropower – are underdeveloped as energy-extraction technologies. We need something to bridge the gap between our current dependence on fossil fuels and mature wind- and hydropower-generation technologies.

Given sufficient government inducements in research and development into green technologies if we could produce more than 40 percent of our energy needs at home using solar, hydroelectric and wind-based systems, and buy in the rest of our electricity needs using power produced in France and the United Kingdom, then our reliance on fossil fuels would largely be at an end by 2050. The pace of change in this area is significantly slower than many believe. The energy technologies the new, green energy-generation methods are designed to replace – oil, coal and gas – are the bedrock of every economy on Earth. Replacing them will take some time. The economy will only retool slowly to incorporate the new power-production technologies, particularly in transport and industry, and only as new plants and vehicles become obsolete.

FACTOID: Carbon fuels presently supply 83 percent of all energy use, with the rest obtained from hydropower (6 percent), biomass (3 percent), nuclear (6 percent) and wind and solar (2 percent). Therefore, renewable energy (excluding nuclear) totals 11 percent, and alternative energy is 17 percent. Hydropower is unlikely to grow significantly because most rivers in developed nations are harnessed, so growth must come from wind, solar, biomass and nuclear. Total energy costs in the US are about $600 billion per year. In 2009, renewable energy was growing by 50 percent per year. (Source: Clean Energy Trends 2009)

Pollution is the price of development, the price of a vibrant economy and the price of a growing middle class. But can the nation afford this new middle class? It's fair to say that nuclear power isn't the solution anyone would want in an ideal world, but there is no solution in the medium term without it, as we transition away from solutions based on fossil fuel-based power. Those electric cars won't charge themselves.

Notwithstanding all of the above, I'm not a fan of nuclear power, and I don't think that Ireland needs its own nuclear power plant. First, we don't have the expertise to build one. Buying in French, British or Japanese technology means transferring billions of euro from Irish taxpayers to French, British or Japanese companies – and all before the plant lights a single bulb. The costs of such a development far out-weigh the benefits – especially when new, cheaper nuclear power plants are being constructed by our neighbours and fellow EU members.

There are ways to buy power produced using nuclear reactors from abroad. A €30 billion investment in nuclear power will take place in the UK in the next ten years. This power will need buyers. If the power is priced properly, Ireland might be in a position to purchase the benefits of nuclear power without incurring many of the costs associated with it – by purchasing power generated by UK nuclear plants through an underwater electrical inter-connector between Ireland and the UK. We could open up our electricity markets and reduce the price of living and the price of doing business in Ireland as a result. A global market for energy is just around the corner, and as Ireland becomes more and more developed, we will need to position ourselves to take account of – and advantage of – these changing trends.

In the next chapter, we'll look at Ireland's economy and society: what changes might we see when we factor in an ageing population, an increasingly secular society, persistent energy issues, and climate change?

DOUBLE-BILL TROUBLE

1 May 2050

Jack Murphy runs his hands through his thinning hair as he stares at his electricity bill. He thinks the bill is too small. He must call someone, but not right now.

Jack's house sells electricity back to the power grid in the summer months, because his well-insulated home has solar panels built into the glass, generating more than enough power for his home.

Thanks to the lucrative sale of a previous business, Jack and his family can afford to live in the hills over-looking Dublin, giving the family immunity from the flooding around Dublin's docklands and the south county, but not protecting Jack from the sight of his lawn as a swamp in the winter and spring, thanks to the rain, or having to water his scorched lawn from June to September every year, which costs him a fortune in water rates. It's worth it for the view, he tells himself. Jack's office also gets a monthly payment, which he's going to query. Because Jack's business, like many businesses, relies on large server farms, which produce large amounts of heat, John's building pumps that heat into a nearby apartment block to heat water and produce power. This reduces his local taxes and his heating bill. Someone's going to get roared at.

When he was a student in the late 2030s, Jack lived in Limerick, in an apartment block close to the docks. The apartment was flooded regularly, and he promised himself that his family would not have to deal with similar disruption. When he could afford it, Jack bought on 'preferred' land, zoned by the county council as less likely to be affected by climate change in general, and flooding in particular. Jack feels as though the house was a good investment, right up until he sees his summer water bill, levied by the council, flash up on his screen. He sighs, and runs his hands through his thinning hair, one more time.

Maeve calls. She wants to talk. She says she's sorry for getting upset, and Jack apologises. Jack asks if she has heard from her boyfriend, Patrick, who hasn't spoken to her in several weeks now. She says she has, and that he's going to come over tonight. Jack is happy she's called to check with him about it, and even though he secretly wants to rip Patrick's head off for his behaviour, he agrees. He'll even cook. Maeve thanks him profusely. They both know Sarah is the worst cook in Ireland. She'd burn cornflakes. If Jack didn't agree, Patrick would be poisoned for sure. Jack tells the fridge to buy in some vegetables, there will be one more for dinner.

FACTOID: England is building off-shore wind farms which will house 6,000 turbines, and Germany is building 16,000 turbines. Germany and Denmark expect to derive half of their energy from wind soon. European wind power overall grew fifty-fold from 1990 to 2002. Broadstar Wind Systems has developed a smaller wind turbine, selling for $250,000, that delivers power for below $1/watt – a figure that is unrivalled in the field. Wind power in North Dakota, Kansas, Texas and other US states alone could provide all of America's energy needs. China is building a wind turbine that is levitated by magnets to reduce friction; this is expected to increase generating capacity by 20 percent and reduce costs by 50 percent. (Source: Give Green, 11/26/07). Experts estimate that wind power could supply 12 percent of the world's energy needs by 2020. The US Department of Energy thinks that wind could provide 20 percent of electricity by 2030. (Source: Smithsonian, July 2008)

7

PEOPLE, PRODUCTION AND THE NATURE OF WORK

Ask anyone what the greatest invention of the twentieth century was. They'll say 'penicillin' or 'nuclear power' or 'relativity' or 'Britney Spears'.

They won't say 'ammonia synthesis'.

The greatest invention of the twentieth century is a chemical trick called the Haber-Bosch process[1]. This process is used in the production of ammonia, which is a key ingredient of fertilisers. Doctors Haber and Bosch both received the Nobel Prize for their work. Their invention allowed for more intensive agricultural development, which created food for billions, and detonated a population explosion which took the Earth's human population from 1.6 billion in 1900 to more than 6 billion in the year 2000.

The scale of the Haber-Bosch process and its usage can't be overstated: the process produces 100 million tons of nitrogen fertiliser per year. 3–5 percent of world natural gas production is consumed in the Haber process (that's around

2 percent of the world's annual energy supply). That fertiliser is responsible for sustaining at least one-third of the Earth's population.

Throughout the twentieth century, advances like the Haber-Bosch process have benefited Ireland, as they have the world, allowing for a rapid expansion in Ireland's population.

This chapter tells a story about how increasing the numbers of people in Ireland will change the types of work we do to enrich our lives. In fact, the nature of work itself will change, because we will be a rich nation operating in a truly global marketplace. Chapter 3 described Ireland's future in terms of our society's approach to education and creativity, and showed Ireland requires a rewriting of the rules of mass education. The reason for this rewriting is to adapt tomorrow's graduates to the requirements of industry. Because the nature of work will change, the nature of what it means to be educated and fit for the purpose of work will have to change also.

FACTOID: Ireland has a special connection to the Haber-Bosch process: we export fertilisers in large quantities, and of course we've benefited from increased efficiencies in agriculture, because our food is now more plentiful, and cheaper. Fertilisers are a double-edged sword, however. Ireland's groundwater is now being poisoned, partly by the overuse of these fertilisers.

Two phrases describe Ireland's population before the Celtic Tiger years: 'emigration' and 'large families'. After the Famine years of the 1840s and 1850s, the Irish population declined steadily, from 8 million in 1841 to around 3 million in 1961. Our population has been on a slow path upward since 1961. We were cruising at a population height of 3.88 million people in 2002. Forecasts for Ireland's population range from 4.6 million to nearly 7 million in 2050.

In the future, Ireland will contain more old people than younger people. Statisticians call this phenomenon the 'greying' of a society. The number of people in the 'working' age group of fifteen to sixty-four will be almost the same, when we compare Ireland in 2009 and Ireland in 2050. The number of people over sixty-five will have trebled. By 2050, Ireland – along with virtually every advanced industrial country – will be losing population at a dramatic rate, as those who die are replaced at a slower rate by newborns. This is because women are having fewer and fewer children each year.

Demographers use statistics like these to study how and why populations change over time. Because demographic forces have played such a key role in Ireland's history, and will continue to do so, it is worth putting in historical perspective the demographic trends of which Ireland will be part.

Between 1750 and 1950, the world's population expanded from around 1 billion to around 3 billion people, in part because of the increased availability of food thanks to the Haber-Bosch process, and also because of sharp decreases in infant mortality and increased life expectancies, thanks to improved hygiene, and advances in public-health medicine.

Turning briefly to the global population for some context, between 1950 and 2000, as the benefits of economic progress spread throughout the globe, the Earth's population doubled again, to over 6 billion people today. The United Nations forecasts that between now and 2050, the global population will grow, but only by about 50 percent. Advanced industrial economies like the USA, Germany, Italy and the UK will see dramatic declines in their populations over this period.

Coming back to Ireland, let's focus briefly on an extremely important number: 2.1. On average, 2.1 is the number of children a nation needs to have, per woman, to maintain a stable population. Anything above 2.1 children per woman, and the population of the country will grow. Anything below 2.1, and the population will shrink. Ireland's fertility rate right now is 1.9. Our population is beginning to decline.

In 1970, on average, women had 4.5 children each across the globe. In 2000, the number had dropped to 2.7 – and that's the worldwide average. Looking ahead to 2050, United Nations statisticians estimate that worldwide, we'll see an average of between 2.05 and 1.6 live births per woman on Earth, meaning that the world's population may stabilise around 10 billion, or go into decline.

Looking at the developed nations of the world, we see an even more dramatic decline from 1950 to 2000. Countries like Italy, Germany and Japan are experiencing this decline *today*, where an ageing workforce collides with a declining birth rate to create social, political and economic upheaval. Total fertility rates in 2005 were as low as 1.3 children per woman in Italy, Spain, Germany and Japan. Governments in these countries are only now implementing policies to try to encourage women to have more babies, to stave off a nightmare scenario where there are too few young people in work to provide adequate funding for the newly retired, and the budget shortfall bankrupts the nation.

Even though Ireland is going to experience the population decline I've described above, we will fare better than other rich nations, and our children will reap the benefits of a demand for their skills internationally, because other nations will not have the same number of young people we will have. Forecasts are for a fertility rate in Ireland of 1.65 in 2041, still well above the forecasts for other EU countries.

So even though we will be producing less people in 2050, we will still be producing more people than other countries, and the people we produced in the early 2000s will still be around – and will be in demand. This factor is very important in what follows.

During the Celtic Tiger years, one of the factors that made Ireland so attractive to foreign companies was the relative youth and high educational level of our population. The Irish labour market in the 1980s and 1990s was remarkable, in that, as an employer, you could find lots of highly qualified young workers who would accept wages which would not push inflation up too much. We will see a version of that attractiveness in the Irish labour market between 2025 and 2035, as our children graduate from colleges and take their places in a global labour market which is experiencing shortages of talented workers.

The labour market itself will have changed, however. First, retirement ages will increase (perhaps to seventy-five) by 2040. Better nutrition, health care and working conditions will allow workers to be productive for longer. Governments will want to limit the expansion of the pensions burden, and moving the retirement goalposts is one way to do this.

Second, the notion of a job for life will have evaporated, as careers will now span sixty years or more. Multiple careers, interspersed with periods of retraining, will be the norm. This implies dislocation, as families adjust to shifts in working patterns. A year here, two years there, and so on.

Third, more and more women will enter the labour market, find jobs, and still produce children. Changes in women's status over the last three decades have been a major determinant of their decision to have more – or fewer – children. Just two generations ago, it was normal for an Irish woman to have between four and six babies. Now, women have to choose whether to have a career outside the home, and whether to have children. Recent research has shown that in most developed countries, women, whether they are working or not, still do most of the housework (and most of the childminding) when they are not at work. Women also earn less than men, on average, though this gap is closing. So the number of children must go down: women have less and less time to care for their children, because now they have jobs and *still* have houses to run. Perhaps not coincidentally, Italy, Spain, Germany and Japan, where men do the smallest fraction of the household duties and child care, are also the high-income countries with the lowest fertility rate.

Living standards in Ireland have adjusted, so that middle-class households require two incomes to keep up with the Joneses. The demand for women in the labour market will not go away – nor, I believe, will most women want to return to the home. I think we are in an intermediate phase, where, as women's incomes become more and more necessary to maintain the living standard of the average household, their needs will begin to be catered for more, and they will assert those needs to a greater extent.

Put simply, the lads will do more of the housework, and more of the childminding. And although it might seem strange, this will result in more kids, *and* more jobs. We can see these effects in Sweden today, where men often take six months off work to mind their newborn children, while their wives return to work.

As Irish men begin to share more of the child-rearing duties, the fertility level will go up again. Not dramatically, and not to the same levels as before women entered the labour market en masse, but enough to ensure that our population levels remain at or above the European average.

Health care services, especially care for the elderly, and information technologies will be the boom industries in the coming decades in Ireland. We'll look at the implications of an older society on health care in Chapter 9.

WHITHER THE PENSIONS POT? TO THE NEW POSSESSOR CLASSES

In Ireland, through the boom years, we prudently began putting 1 percent of our nation's output into the National Pension Reserve Fund to begin to address the problem of a rapidly ageing society. Now, much of the pension reserve has been committed to reducing the fallout of the collapse of our financial sector after the bursting of the construction bubble. That fund will have to be rebuilt but, as I'll argue in the final chapter, Irish people of our generation must look to themselves, and not to the government, for adequate pension provision to maintain our standards of living when we are older.

Because people will continually re-train and re-contract their labour, emphasis will have to be placed on personal saving and investment. Each person's work will have to be paid for almost on a piecework basis, with very defined contracts and hours of work for different projects. The relationship between employer and employee will be purely mercenary, with each contracting for labour on a very fixed (and very temporary) basis. The average worker will have to accept that, because of the temporary and rather atomistic nature of the labour market, they will probably spend part of their time unemployed or retraining.

The other factor which might push up the savings rate in Irish society is the larger number of middle-aged and older workers. Older people tend to rely more on savings rather than income from work. Increased worker mobility through personal travel, as well as digital exchanges, will further shift the balance in favour of saving, because the more likely people are to change jobs, the more likely they are to need to save to fund the transfer period between those jobs. As savings accumulate and are passed on from one generation to the next, we will see the emergence of a new possessor class in Ireland, one not tied to property or political connections, but whose wealth comes chiefly from investments and new business interests. There is a parallel with Victorian England in this description, where a large and very wealthy upper middle class of professionals, who were not strictly aristocratic, lived off their investments – and in quite some style. These wealthy individuals had to work, but their incomes were increased by returns on different investments, so that their children never needed to think about working – although of course many did work. Thomas Mann's great 1903 essay 'The Child Prodigy' (*Das Wunderkind*) depicts the product of one of these wealthy households, just about to play a concert which everyone already knows will be a success, because his parents are so successful. The novelist Gustav Flaubert's father was a medical doctor, and was able to ensure that his son, a literary genius, would never need to do paid work[2].

Perhaps the children of the new possessor classes will be so lucky.

OLDER SOCIETIES ARE DIFFERENT FROM YOUNGER SOCIETIES

I've shown several times that Ireland's population will begin to age, as fewer young people are born to 'replace' older ones. The notion that Ireland might remain largely the same as a society and culture in the presence of healthier, wealthier and more numerous older people is misplaced. The values of older people will continue to dominate how the Irish economy and society works – meaning that we are likely to see less inflation in Ireland, because older voters will dominate the polls, and will be very hostile to any policy which might whittle away their savings. We'll see lower unemployment, because of a fall in the proportion of people of working age in Ireland. We'll see lower crime, because the young overwhelmingly commit offences, and older people are much less tolerant of crime. There will be a lower tolerance of disorder and of anti-social behaviour, combined with a greater acceptance of authority.

This might sound like a return to the forelock-tugging and petticoat-wearing of an earlier era, but it won't feel that way to the older people in Irish society, because those people will be us. We will simply resist any attempt to change our way of life, and we will have the financial and political muscle to ensure whatever status quo we like. That power might turn out to be very costly for Irish society, because a large and expensive group of older people demanding more from pension reserves and health care services, and which can veto any decrease in their pensions provision, means, in the end, higher taxes for those currently in work, and more political pain for those in power.

Also, because of an increase in their financial, cultural

and political clout, elderly people will see an increase in the legal rights and protections due to them, as well as attaining a more prominent position within our society. Laws will be changed by special-interest groups to favour the elderly, while entertainment will change to reflect their demographic dominance, as the entertainment industry re-tunes itself to reflect the preferences of older people – something which entertainment networks will be able to gauge through ratings, advertising revenues and television licences.

THE YOUTH BULGE

Ireland experienced a population boom in the late 1970s. I am one of the generation economist David McWilliams calls 'the Pope's Children', after the visit by Pope John Paul II in 1978, when the baby boom peaked. When I did the Leaving Certificate in 1996, more than 60,000 people took it that year – a new record.

Closer to the present, births began to increase in the second half of the 1990s, and the rate of increase has been rapid over the past five years. There is a very real possibility that the 1980 peak of 74,000 births may soon be surpassed. In the year to April 2008, there were 72,300 babies born, and Ireland now has the highest birth rate in Europe. Though the increase in the birth rate is probably temporary – a product of our boom years, and the fact that the women in the generation called the Pope's Children are now entering their thirties, meaning that they couldn't postpone having children for much longer – the population 'boom-boom' will leave Ireland in a relatively strong position when the children of the 2000s reach maturity in the 2030s and, in the 2040s, begin having children of their own.

These huge swings in the birth rate are having serious consequences right now for resource allocation, especially in the health and education sectors. Dublin's maternity hospitals are now bursting at the seams, while the educational system will continue to feel the impact of growing numbers of school-age children for years to come – implying a need to resource further the educational sector to cope with the challenges of producing individuals with the ability to compete effectively in world labour markets.

The key question is: will the number of births per woman in Ireland continue to grow in the foreseeable future, or will the numbers drop as far, and as fast, as the growth rate of the economy? No one can be sure. Population projections are notoriously imprecise, but the most up-to-date forecasts have Ireland experiencing a 'youth bulge' of the Pope's *Grand*children around 2025, as those born in the early years of the twenty-first century become adults, owners and earners. Sadly, it seems that the youth bulge won't be enough to stave off the long-term greying of Irish society, as more and more of us survive (and continue to be productive) well into our seventies, but it will provide us with a window of time in which to enrich the nation – if we begin to prepare for it soon. Moving on from population effects, what changes can be seen in the Irish economy today, and for the future?

IRELAND'S ECONOMY IN TRANSITION

Chapter 2 described how Ireland has just transitioned from a developing economy based on light manufacturing and agriculture to a developed one, complete with an explosive period of growth known as the Celtic Tiger years, a housing boom – and bust – and the miseries attendant on a bust. The economy of Ireland has changed dramatically since 1950. But change is nothing new: our economy has seen large-scale structural change dominate the social, political and economic landscape for more than fifteen years.

The importance of agriculture, lower-skilled occupations and services (except those relating to construction) and light industry has steadily diminished over this period, while growth in services – particularly financial services – is seen as the engine of economic development. We are still recognisably Ireland, however profound these changes have been, in the same way as you are recognisably yourself, though you have grown older, and almost every cell in your body has been replaced in the last five years. In this chapter, let's talk about the likely effects of the long-term structural changes on Ireland's economy, looking forward two generations.

The economy of Ireland in 2050 will have many of the same features our economy today has, as today's economy contains many of the features the Irish economy had in 1960. We will see profound structural change in the intervening years between now and 2050, but the necessities of life, which the economy exists to try and satisfy, will not change. Exactly how those necessities are satisfied will change, and what our grandchildren define as a 'necessity' will change, and change utterly, thanks to high-tech consumerism, environmental challenges, and simple cost.

Chapter 2 showed that Ireland exists in an interconnected network of trading partners. We provide a gateway for US products to Europe, and vice versa. Take the market for semiconductors, a component in electronic design. Ireland imported €217 million worth of these products from the US in 2008, and exported €380 million worth of semiconductors *back* to the US. What was Ireland's role in this process? We provided cheap, highly skilled labour, high-quality production facilities, and low-taxation strictures for companies to locate here, making the decision to invest in Ireland a sound one, as long as we remained cheaper than our competitors. We remained part of the production process, but only a small part of an otherwise US-directed industry. There are many examples of highly globalised, but US-directed, industries.

Take Mattel's Barbie doll product. Barbie is one of the most recognised brands on Earth, and the design and manufacture of the doll just about spans the globe. From the design of a new Barbie doll in the US, to the sourcing of materials from the US, China, Saudi Arabia, Hong Kong, Taiwan and Japan, the making of Barbie is a truly global phenomenon. It has always been like this: though Barbie is owned and developed by US toy giant Mattel, the dolls have never been manufactured in the US. Beginning in 1959, Barbie has been produced in Japan, and it is now produced in Indonesia and China. There is one factory each in Indonesia and Malaysia and two factories in China. In China, the Meitai factory is located in Dongguan, and the Zhongmei factory is in Nanhai. The Meitai plant makes the plastic dolls and the clothes while the Zhongmei plant makes only the dolls. Each of these Chinese factories have 5,500 workers. Barbie is a global product, and the design and branding of the doll is completely divorced from the production and distribution. So it will be with many Irish products in the future: we will be designers, marketers and fabricators, but in specialised niche markets, and usually not all of these things for a particular product at once. The nature of work will have changed. We will not be the cheapest around, either.

The advantages of being relatively cheap are fleeting. As the number of people in employment rises, they start buying houses, cars, fridges and a host of other products and services. When businesses start seeing new customers coming through their doors demanding more of the products they have to sell, inevitably the price of what the businesses sell will go up as they increase their mark-ups. It's human nature. When prices go up, employees begin asking for wage increases to maintain their standard of living. Suddenly, the economy begins to look less inviting to outside investors, because the rate of wage increases is being matched by increases in inflation, making the economy relatively more expensive. What once attracted outside investors is gone. The only way to retrieve the cost advantages we once enjoyed is through a reduction in living standards: wages have to fall through unemployment and wage bargaining, and with the fall in wages, the prices of goods and services must decrease. We could choose to begin that cycle again, on a race to the bottom of the pile of Western industrialised countries in terms of our living standards. This is the lesson of the 2002–07 boom.

Or we could choose to develop further.

As a country, we have reached the last rung of a ladder we began climbing in the late 1960s. Seán Lemass, our then Taoiseach, set out a framework for export-led growth, where we would enrich ourselves as a nation by selling things to other people. But who made those things? Anyone but us. The things were made elsewhere, and packaged, or assembled, or sold from, here. Only rarely was Ireland chosen as the site of the production of all aspects of a good or service, and even then the profits made by the company were taken out of Ireland to the home country. Inevitably, Ireland was used as a gateway to Europe from the US, or vice versa. Rather than being a hub for trade, we were a lay-by. The benefits of this arrangement for the export-led approach are obvious: increased employment for an up-skilled workforce, increased female participation in the labour market, higher wages, and increased demand for 'Irish' products abroad – all of it resulting in high growth. An export-led Celtic Tiger economy was born in the early 1990s, the result of the combination of an opening up of trade with the EU thanks to the Single Market programme begun in 1992, the freeing up of air transport, a booming US economy in the Clinton era thanks to the explosion in dot-com companies, historically low interest rates allowing for free transfers of money to and from Ireland through our financial services sector, and a relatively stable international political climate thanks to the dissolution of the Soviet Union leaving the United States as the world's only superpower.

Effectively, Ireland responded to the opening up of world trade by becoming one of the most open economies in the world. We prospered as the international economy prospered. When it faltered, in 2007, so did we.

JOBS WILL CHANGE, WORK WILL NOT

My mother gave my oldest son some of the books I read as a child the other day. One of these books has cartoon animals dressed up, representing various occupations. The book's thick, hard pages show us a mouse dressed as a firefighter, a doctor-cat in a white coat (complete with a stethoscope for a collar), a dog dressed as a baker, and so on.

If the publishers of the children's book decided to update the book for all the new jobs that have been created in the last twenty years, the mouse, cat and dog would all be pictured sitting at a laptop, headphones on, Googling stuff, sipping coffee – and writing snarky comments on blogs instead of working.

It is a common assertion that the nature of work has changed, and will continue to change, as businesses become smaller, more Web-aware, and more niche-orientated. Businesses will fail more often, because of the challenges thrown up by the need to compete in a global marketplace. Failure will become endemic in business culture, and will be seen as market feedback rather than an indictment of the talent of the men and women running the business.

Swings in the integration of global markets for labour mean that shortages of workers in countries like the US by 2030 will be met by increased immigration of workers.

Ireland will be in a unique position to take advantage of this scarcity of talented labour – but only if we can equip our educational institutions to meet the coming demand for highly skilled, highly mobile, competent workers.

How will work change? I would assert that, fundamentally, work will not change. Most work will continue to be unpleasant and poorly paid, relative to the effort we feel we put into our jobs, and our bosses will still be idiots. The only real difference is that *we* will be the bosses. In a globally connected world, rich Irish people will be able to invest their money in businesses and ventures all over the world, and locally. We will be capitalists and entrepreneurs, as well as workers.

As economies mature, the general pattern seems to be that people are drawn off the land by the promise of a better life in cities[3]. These 'economic migrants' take jobs working at whatever industry happens to be booming at the moment and demanding more and more workers. Factories, hotels, bars and construction sites, as well as a myriad of support services around the booming industry absorb these workers. These people work, consume and save their wages, get older, marry, and have children. They buy property. The workers' children spend longer in education, and get better jobs than their parents had. The children of the migrants use their education to get better jobs. The cycle continues over time and, generation after generation, the economy develops, requiring more highly educated people to run ever more highly specialised, more productive processes, and to provide new and more efficient services.

Think about someone working in a call centre in 2009. This work is seen as low-skilled, in the sense that call-centre jobs can be readily outsourced to developing nations, where the average educational level (and correspondingly, the wage) is lower.

Now think about the skills someone working in a call centre needs. Call-centre operators need to be able to read, to write, to operate a telephone, to work with a computer, and to use specialised software – all while talking to different people, hopefully solving problems or giving customers information. Working in a call centre with today's technologies would have been beyond all but the most highly educated people even twenty-five years ago. Yet today, call-centre work is seen as 'low skilled'.

We saw in the previous chapters that, in 2050, the economy of Ireland will be different from the one we see today, especially in how the workers are educated, the types of industries they find themselves in, and even who will pay them. Our grandchildren will have a different conception of what it means to 'work' and produce, and they will have to make decisions about what to produce and consume which are both easier and more difficult than ours today.

Take the choice of where to live. The Irish family of 2050 will have to take transport times into account, where to park their car (if they have one), where to locate their businesses, and what type of house to purchase or rent. Irish people have, for generations, relied on purchasing housing as a means to get on to the 'property ladder' and become wealthy. Today, as we suffer through a deep slump in the market for housing and commercial property, we may no longer see owning property as a guaranteed route to personal wealth and advancement. In fact, it may take fifteen years for the property market in Ireland to reach the heights it saw in 2006 and 2007. But the focus of this book is the next forty years. I think we will see another housing and construction boom in Ireland in the early 2020s, as a larger, older population demands different types of residences, and as a more modern infrastructure is built to replace our existing roads, railways and sea links.

In summary, we will see large changes in the way the labour market works in advanced societies like Ireland. Obviously, retirement ages will have to rise to cope with the existence and relative health of a large number of older workers. Female labour market participation rates will climb to near-parity with male participation rates. Part-time working will increase; university students, who are already expected to work part-time during term, may see the demand for their services rise so fast that college and universities will largely become the 'part-time' element in their lives. Greater efforts will be made to mobilise the unemployed, and retraining, perhaps several times in a career, will become the norm. Workers will be rootless, and largely unorganised by unions. There will be an increase in voluntary labour and volunteering in general as people seek fulfilment outside the normal worker-employer relationships, and there will be ever more pressure on young people to learn marketable skills and acquire 'training' in place of a more general education.

Some of the features I've noted above are already taking place, and many will continue to drive change in the labour market for decades to come[4].

FACTOID: Markets are penetrating the economy even more deeply because the very nature of today's knowledge-driven world is far too complex for any other coordination system. As the information technology revolution automates routine jobs, and others are outsourced or offshored, what's left of corporate operations is basically entrepreneurial and bureaucratic. Now that business units can operate anywhere using IT, it is almost impossible to supervise people closely. In 2008, Best Buy, an electronics retailer, moved to a 'results only' system that allows employees to choose when, where and how they work as long as they produce to a given target. Google uses teams to manage each project as a small internal venture, while the company really serves as an internal venture-capital firm, placing bets on the best projects. Nokia uses autonomous business units to launch new phones each year. At IBM, 42 percent of employees do not have offices, and one-third of all AT&T managers are free to 'telework' from home, the client's office, or wherever they choose. The result is that large corporations are fragmenting into far-flung constellations of 'internal enterprises', operating in a web of economic markets. This trend is set to continue.

INNOVATION AND THE IRISH ECONOMY

Innovation only occurs when the conditions are correct: you need a stable democracy, and enough space for the entrepreneur to attempt something, and you need to allow people to fail more easily, to see failure as feedback from which one learns rather than as an admission of uselessness. This is something that Irish people, in Ireland, are not good at, but virtually everywhere else in the world, Irish entrepreneurs do extremely well.

What is the innovation economy, and why does it matter for our kids? The innovation economy is that part of the economy driven by small and medium enterprises which fuse global capital and labour resources with technology to create new products primarily built on intellectual property. Innovation is simply a catch-all term for the development of some service, process, device or product which changes the manner in which businesses and countries do what they do. Why does that matter? The simple production of basic goods does not make a country rich any more; producing goods and services of a higher quality, in a more efficient manner, using the most ecologically responsible methods, does. Ireland needs to come up with these more efficient processes and products, and to do so, it needs to innovate. In short, Ireland needs to become an innovation economy.

Is Ireland an innovation economy today? Yes, but only in patches. We see innovation and invention in high-tech industries, but not within the 'built' environment, for example. The Irish construction industry is largely a craft-based industry rather than one based on the high-precision (and high-value) manufacturing processes employed by German and Japanese house-builders.

Industries in which an innovation economy are most likely to emerge are pharmaceuticals and health care, energy development, communications, materials science, and entertainment. The reason for this is simple: the returns on a big innovation in any of these industries are potentially enormous, so a great deal of effort will be devoted to research and development, and to market-testing new products and services in these industries. Most of this research will fail; some will not. The research that allows a marketable product to be developed will flourish, and create new sub-industries underneath it.

Take the MP3 player, for example. This is a simple fusion of battery-powered hard-drive technology to liquid-crystal displays. The real innovation comes in the software, which allows the music to be transferred, and the distribution of the music using the web, paid for (when it *is* paid for) by credit cards using secure micro-payment facilities. A market for digital downloads now exists where, five years ago, there was nothing. As I write, Apple's iTunes online store has just sold its 8 billionth song. Here, in the entertainment sphere, the business model has had to change to take account of so-called 'disruptive' technologies like internet distribution and costless copying. A sign of the times we live in and the changes we are likely to see in the next ten to twenty years, the best-selling MP3 album at Amazon in 2008 was Nine Inch Nails' *Ghosts I-IV*, which was released free under a Creative Commons licence. Creative Commons means that anyone can take the material being sold, legally download it from any file-sharing network, and remix, copy, redistribute and remake the songs. But the customers didn't do that. Fans of the music bought the album, knowing that doing so would contribute directly to the artist and support their career.

Smart materials and precision prefabricated construction environments will likewise remake the construction industry in the years to come, because the potential profits are so large. The notion of passive survivability – that buildings ought to be designed to promote the survival of their users in adverse situations like hurricanes – is remaking materials science. For instance, companies are developing nails which are 50 percent more resistant to strain than regular nails. This means that the building will be stronger, last longer, and be more sustainable, as it will require less maintenance; lives will be saved as a result. The US army has developed bomb-proof wallpaper. This product, a kind of tape, is used to coat the interior sides of exterior walls in order to absorb the shock of a blast, protecting the occupants from flying concrete and metal turned into projectiles. In 2008, a new method of handling wood fibres so that cellulose fibres are undamaged was developed. Mechanical tests show that undamaged cellulose paper has a tensile strength of 214 megapascals, making it stronger than cast iron (130 MPa) and almost as strong as structural steel (250 MPa). This would be a cheap way to increase the strength of construction material. As these technologies develop, become cheaper, and hence become widely adopted, expect revolutions in architecture, construction, and sustainable buildings.

Industries will grow, develop, die, and remake themselves in the next forty years. Forecasting which ones will thrive is very difficult, but the broad trends are fairly easy to predict.

What about individual companies and businesses in Ireland?

FACTOID: Graphene is a material that consists of a sheet of carbon molecules organised into a grid one atom thick. This material has unusual properties, making it an ideal replacement for silicon chips. It conducts electricity a hundred times faster than silicon at room temperatures. Graphene could also be used as an ultra-light, high-strength structural material for cars and especially aircraft, as it is five hundred times stronger than steel at one-tenth the weight. Nanorods have been compressed under high temperature to produce the strongest material known, able to scratch diamonds. Researchers have used printing techniques to combine nanotubes, nanowires, silicon and other materials to build multilayered chips that combine high-performance optical and electronic functions. Toyota has developed an unusual alloy of four metals that can stretch to twice its length and bend at right angles. Apollo Diamond Company has developed a process to make cheap artificial diamonds that could replace silicon for superior computer chips. A researcher has synthesised spider's silk, creating fibres that are five times as strong as steel and three times as tough as synthetic fabrics.

FAIL

1 June 2050

Jack Murphy has a quote from George Bernard Shaw over his desk. The quote reads: 'A life spent making mistakes is not only more honourable but more useful than a life spent in doing nothing.' Jack thinks this quote sums up his working life. Jack's businesses have been failing and succeeding for nearly twenty years now, and he is already looking at start-up number fifteen.

FAILING CONSTRUCTIVELY

In Chapter 2, I argued that, as a nation, we need to fail, but fail constructively. Individually, that means setting up businesses as market-based experiments, and using the success or failure of these experiments as guides on what to do next. Constant churning of jobs, roles, capital, people, and their ideas will become the norm. Massive rewards will coexist with spectacular failure.

Building an innovation economy means starting many enterprises which simply don't work. The entrepreneur has to be able to set up a business quickly, protect its intellectual property, and develop the core ideas, products and services of the business in order to make a profit in an uncertain environment. Most of these businesses are going to fail, and fail quickly. Silicon Valley in the late 1990s is an example, in bubble form, of the type of wealth creation which can accompany idea generation on a vast scale. The dot-com boom was a bubble, but I would argue that the industry model represented by small start-ups like Google (a company which was set up as recently as 1998) and Netscape (now the Mozilla Foundation) gives us the blueprint for the organisation of the future.

The Mozilla Corporation has seventy full-time employees, and a developer network of more than two hundred thousand unpaid volunteers, who contribute time and expertise to make the products produced by Mozilla (including the internet browser Firefox, which, at the time of writing, has a 20 percent market share) better and more cutting-edge. Mozilla Corp. mainly produces a product which is free: the Firefox browser has been downloaded more than 200 million times, and no one has ever paid for it.

Mozilla can't grow in a 'normal' fashion, because its funding model is not geared towards the maximisation of shareholder value. The Mozilla Corporation is actually a subset of the Mozilla Foundation. The Mozilla Corporation is responsible for productising and distributing Firefox, Thunderbird, and related branded products built on the Mozilla open-source code base. The Mozilla Corporation's mission, shared by that of the Mozilla Foundation, is to promote choice and innovation on the internet.

The Mozilla Corporation offers no monetary rewards to the community of developers who maintain its code base. The incentives for an individual to donate their time are simple recognition, or to see if they can change something in the code which annoys them. Individual volunteers usually begin their participation in the project as a way to 'scratch their own itch', for example by reporting or, in some cases, fixing bugs that affect them, or even developing new Mozilla code or new Firefox extensions to perform some function which is important to them. Over time, project participants may become professionally involved in Mozilla-related development, for example by working for one of the many corporations sponsoring Mozilla development, or by starting their own Mozilla-related businesses.

The Mozilla Corporation is an example of a new type of organisation, which is best suited to producing innovative products that millions of people will use on a daily basis. These organisations are small, they outsource a huge amount of their workload, and they create new products, which they give away for nothing, or almost nothing.

At first, the modern profit-centred organisation is very small, unless it gets very big. This might seem nonsensical. Imagine a company that wants to make a new type of imaging equipment. A technology-savvy workforce is required to manufacture the equipment when it has been designed, but true creatives are required to produce the design. Workers who can think for themselves, who can work remotely or in collaboration, and who can turn an outline brief ('make a better nail') into a marketable product will be valued and, consequently, rewarded.

In this chapter, we have seen that Irish workers will be in demand across the globe, Irish businesses will largely outsource their functions (or become part of another firm's outsourcing activities), and wealthy Irish entrepreneurs will be free to invest (and fail) across the globe. In the next chapter, we'll look at the future of Ireland's cities, towns and transport systems.

8

INCUBATORS OF APATHY, DISCONNECTION AND DELIRIUM? OUR ROADS, OUR CITIES AND OUR SUBURBS

YOU ARE JUST GOING TO *LOVE* PAYING FOR STUFF THAT USED TO BE FREE

Road pricing entails charging someone to use a piece of road at a particular time. By making road users to incur a cost, you force them to choose whether they really want to drive at that particular time. Congestion is reduced for everyone who does actually need to use the road, which is a scarce resource, at that time. If you don't want to pay, stay at home and do something more fun than sit in traffic, or get to where you want to go by bike, train, magic carpet, or whatever. If you do pay, the money (ideally) goes to fund better roads in the future. Everyone wins.

Road pricing is not a new idea. To end the scourge of traffic congestion, Julius Caesar banned most carts from the streets of ancient Rome during daylight hours. The result? Roman traffic jams shifted from midday to dusk, choking access to one of Western civilisation's first cities just as the sun went down. People react to changing incentives.

Readers who live in large cities like Dublin, Cork and Belfast today probably need little convincing that traffic congestion is personally frustrating and socially wasteful – and perpetually on the rise[1]. As the population grows and the effects of climate change manifest themselves ever more strongly, population densities in major urban areas will increase, traffic congestion will continue to rise, and road pricing will become the norm in non-residential areas.

The key to seeing road pricing as a benefit is to see it as saving everyone time in the end. The Texas Transportation Institute[2] estimated that the average American urban traveller lost nearly one full workweek to congestion in 2005. And congestion is getting worse, not better: urban travellers in the same city in 1982 were delayed only fourteen hours that year. As Ireland's urban population grows and changes its composition from primarily younger to primarily older people, the traffic problems that dog the development of all our cities will only get worse. Congestion, like pollution, is one of the costs of development.

Cities and suburbs provide the context for congestion problems. For the first time in human history, the majority of people reside in cities. Our species evolved to live expansively, in small, mobile tribes[3]. The migration from the land to cities marked a dramatic, and irreversible, shift away from this pattern[4].

Instead of inhabiting wide-open spaces, we are crowded

into concrete shapes, living in (sometimes quite nice) boxes, surrounded by buses, taxis, traffic, fumes – and millions of strangers. The city is the modern savannah, and Ireland's development will take place largely in the shadow of the development of Dublin, Limerick, Cork and Galway. That is, if you can get into these cities to do your shopping easily, and run your business cost-effectively.

For decades, economists and other transportation thinkers have advocated imposing tolls that vary according to congestion levels on urban roadways. The idea is: as congestion increases, raise the toll until the congestion goes away.

Today, an electronically collected toll system charges drivers more to use the most congested roads at the most congested times. As with airline tickets, prices can be cheaper at off-peak times, and motorists are forced either to wait or to pay. Congestion charges can apply to, say, one lane, or one part of the road. In this case, the rest of the road remains crowded and congested.

The concept of road pricing sounds, and has always sounded, like a scheme drawn up by moustache-twirling bureaucrats and their academic apologists (i.e. people like me) to fleece the average driver out of their hard-earned cash. The notion of yet more government-sponsored drains on their incomes grates on most Irish ears.

The natural reaction is: why should drivers have to pay to use roads their taxes have already paid to build? Won't the remaining free roads be swamped as drivers are forced off the tolled roads? Won't the working class and the poor be the victims here, as the tolled routes turn into 'Lexus lanes'? And besides, adopting this policy would mean listening to economists, and who wants to do that?

To make tolling truly effective, the price must be right.

Too high a price drives away too many cars, and the road does not function at its most efficient capacity. Too low a price, and congestion isn't reduced enough.

The best solution is to vary the tolls in real time based on an analysis of current traffic conditions. Pilot toll projects on roads have used sensors embedded in the pavement, and placed on the cars themselves, to monitor the numbers – and speeds – of vehicles using the facility. In London, where a crude form of congestion pricing has been in effect for several years now, they have seen a 30 percent average drop in congestion, a 37 percent average increase in traffic speed, a 12 percent drop in particulate matter and nitrogen oxide, and a 20 percent decrease in fossil fuel consumption and carbon dioxide (CO_2) emissions. All of which is good for the individual motorist as well as for society in general.

The other barrier to using road pricing is who chooses the price, and who gets the revenue. Public Private Partnerships (PPPs) have been in fashion for some time in Irish public life, but they have yet to produce a demonstratively beneficial effect on Irish society.

Since PPPs were launched in Ireland almost ten years ago, proponents have argued that they yield better value for money than traditional procurement methods. But this argument was largely based on the expectation that, under PPPs, the private sector would take on risks that they would not normally run under traditional procurement. Risk transfer, we are told, creates incentives for private contractors to complete projects on time as well as ensuring that they provide quality services and value for money. If projects are not completed on time, the private sector does not get paid. If services offered are not in accordance with the standards specified in detailed contracts, the private sector runs the risk of incurring penalties.

As we have seen in Chapter 3, in 2050 our notion of personal privacy will be a thing of the distant past. Individual road pricing will be taken to an astounding level. With sensors allowing precise control over the individual details of each car, the authorities will index the toll to the street value of the vehicle itself in real time, as well as the location on the road of the car at that moment, and the income of the car's owner. As a result, traffic jams may well be a thing of the past by the time our grandchildren learn to drive (or be driven).

FACTOID: Smarter roads kill fewer people. The costs of traffic congestion are enormous, but traffic engineers think that automated highways would improve safety considerably while alleviating congestion. In the USA, average travel speeds on commuter corridors are 36 miles per hour, leading to 5 billion lost working hours, and productivity losses of $50 billion, each year. The total distances that people travelled increased by 65 percent between 1970 and 1990, and is expected to double between 1990 and 2020. Annual delays per traveller increased from 14 hours in 1982 to 38 hours in 2005. Although US highway accident rates are in long-term decline, 6.2 million crashes occured in 2005, causing 43,000 fatalities and 2.6 million injuries, and costing $150 billion in lost time, wasted fuel, and damages. Computer models indicate that automation would double or even triple US highway capacity.

CITIES AND SUBURBS

Ireland's cities are simultaneously both old and new. Dublin, Galway, Cork and Kilkenny have been concentrated settlements of economic activity for hundreds of years, and since

1990 we have seen a near-doubling of the populations of these three cities. The central feature of this development in building activity, and the expansion of Ireland's urban settlements, is the direction in which this development occurred: *out*, not *up*[5]. This increase is common in developed countries. A total of 252 million people – 83.5 percent of all Americans – live in metropolitan areas. That includes 164 million in the fifty-one biggest metro areas – the ones with populations above 1 million.

To get a sense of the scale of the sprawl of suburbia coast to coast in Ireland, go to a computer, and navigate your browser to *http://maps.google.com*. Look at a satellite map of County Dublin and surrounding counties. On an average computer screen (and depending on the size of your hand), suburban sprawl carries the eye from a finger's width beyond the Liffey, all the way down to Wicklow, up to Meath and Cavan, and out west to Kildare and Louth. Dublin city, its natural hinterland, and the new commuter towns of the boom, places like Tullamore, County Offaly. Fuelled by cheap credit and its resultant property boom, we now have suburban developments in previously rural areas. These estates – and their occupants – are here to stay. How Ireland deals with these suburbs will help define the development of our society for the next thirty years[6].

Foreclosures are rising and house prices are dropping rapidly in the suburbs, although the same can, to a lesser extent, be said about apartments in inner-city Dublin and Cork. Traffic is a problem in these areas, as once-small towns with populations in the hundreds now have to cope with a thousand or more new inhabitants in the areas surrounding them – with no increase in service provision.

I live in a small village called Murroe, in County Limerick, in a new housing estate. In 2002, there were 464 houses in Murroe. In 2008, the number was 1604, with the new ones populated mainly by young couples with children – exactly my story. The local school didn't get an extension, so classes will be overcrowded when my eldest son goes to school. The one and only street in the village didn't get any more litter bins, so the town is dirty for the first time in its history. The locals complain that the 'blow-ins' don't salute them in the street. Longtime residents feel that their village is being taken away from them. Thanks to the increase in unemployment, the local postmistress has no time to talk to elderly locals as she once did. There is no playground for the children of newly arrived couples, no amenities for teenagers, and traffic through the village has increased out of all proportion since 2002, I'm told. Increased traffic means increased pollution, the potential for more accidents, and more stress. Crime is on the rise. Murroe experienced its first-ever mugging in December 2008.

'Short-term teething problems', you might say – and you would be right. Over time, services, provided largely by the private market, will expand to cope with the increased demand for them, and people will learn to live anonymously, keep to themselves, and be more wary. Increased levels of isolation will become common. The postmistress will have to be a little more efficient. The local council will build in more bins, and hopefully parents will teach their children not to drop litter. The local park, paid for through donations, will make space for more sporting events.

In the medium term, though, three problems present themselves: access to services, job creation, and societal integration of what might come to be called the 'Youth Bulge'.

ACCESS TO SERVICES

Ireland currently enjoys relatively low levels of income taxes, which pay for relatively low levels of public services, when we compare our public services to those of the UK, France, Germany, Sweden or Norway. But Ireland's taxation regime is changing as we adjust to a new, more austere economic reality. Our public services, in contrast, are not changing. Structurally, many public services remain largely the same as they were in the 1990s; one characteristic dominates them all – queuing.

More people accessing the same services means either that the services become more efficient to cope with increased demand and still supply the same quality of service, the service becomes more efficiently supplied by becoming poorer-quality, or the service remains the same, and just gets slower, with the result that people will wait longer for services they can't pay for directly. Chances are that many of these public services will be in the areas of education, sanitation and sewage, health (especially care for the elderly), information provision, and access to public amenities.

The new suburbia in the hinterland of Ireland's old towns will experience the lack of access to services in the next five to ten years, with the children of these areas being deprived as a result. When I say deprived, I mean impoverished, but in a slight sense. Let me explain. The suburbs will contain the children of Ireland's new middle class. These children will go to schools where the teacher/student ratio is well above European averages. The children will fight for time with the teacher and their assistants, and their learning may be compromised. The sports and social activities available to these children as they grow to adolescence may be lacking, so they will become less and less socialised as a result, and may thus find it hard to become part of society when they leave full-time education. The process I'm writing about affects every child in this fictional suburb, but the marginal child, whose parents don't read to him, who is not particularly gifted educationally, who cannot interact easily with others his own age, and who feels a lack of commitment on the part of society to him, will end up disaffected and detached, and may create problems for this suburb, where none previously existed.

Large-scale unsupported suburban life creates many problems[7]. Several studies have shown that in commuter-belt suburbs around Dublin, levels of attachment to the community are low. Researchers found a rather lonely world there also: most people in suburbs know six to ten people in the area, meaning that they are unable to rely on a large group for help. Only one-third of the people in suburbs belong to voluntary organisations or community groups; activism is quite low in such areas.

Governance, connection, and political representation is, and will remain, a problem, because meaningful government is only possible when people engage with their communities. One simple solution might be to attempt to empower local voluntary organisations, to resource them to help promote civic engagement and thereby reduce the likelihood of civil unrest, disconnection, and isolation. Local authorities must bend to the notion of bringing local residents into a fold where their needs are heard and their complaints listened to.

Like many of the arguments in this book, the need to foster connections between suburban dwellers and their communities is straight from 'for the want of a nail, the shoe was lost, for the want of a shoe, the horse was lost, for the want of a horse, the battle was lost' school of thought. Public services are the nails that hold a society together. By moving large tracts of our growing population to suburbs which have unequal and inefficient access to overcrowded public services like education, health and sports facilities, we ensure that more and more children end up disaffected and alone, on the edges of our society. Through inaction, we will have created a twenty-first-century underclass from the children of the new rich, and they will attempt to damage the society that damaged them.

JOB CREATION IN SUBURBIA

How do we stop our children and grandchildren becoming disaffected in the coming decades? By ensuring that social order prevails, and by promoting prosperity through increased job and investment prospects in the places where we live. If you were from Tullamore in 1990, 'getting ahead' meant travelling to a big city, like Dublin, acquiring an education, and getting a job in one of the large companies there. In 2050, local companies located in the suburbs and tied into training programmes run by universities will develop young people's general and job-specific skill sets close to where they live. When they feel the need to move, they will be able to, from a confident base of hands-on experience and education.

BUILDINGS BUILDING THEMSELVES

Buildings and architecture have changed out of all recognition in the last thirty years, thanks to advances in material science. Now buildings which once required brick and mortar can be made of glass and steel. Concrete itself is changing, with profound effects for the type of buildings we live in, and the type of industrial structures we can produce. The most obvious effect of the new materials being developed relates to their durability. A containment vessel for nuclear waste built to last a hundred years with today's concrete could last up to sixteen thousand years if made with an ultra-high-density (UHD) concrete. UHD concrete could alter structural designs, as well as having enormous environmental implications, because concrete is the most widely produced man-made material on earth: 20 billion tons are produced per year worldwide, with a 5 percent annual increase in this figure. More-durable concrete means that less building material and less frequent renovations will be required in our buildings by 2050.

JACK AND JILL

1 July 2050

Six years ago, overweight and constantly tired, Jack Murphy went to his doctor for some tests. He knows from the genomic history taken at that consultation that he's likely to experience heart problems as he ages. In fact a recent series of tests show Jack is likely to have some form of heart complication in the next eight to ten years. His mother died from a heart attack at sixty years of age. Jack's father was overweight for many years, and is diabetic. Jack needs to eat less red meat Mondays, Thursdays, and Saturdays, and train intermittently as his business schedule allows. His diet is altered to reduce the chances of contracting a range of heart problems. Jack's phone is upgraded to monitor his vital signs, and a genetically tailored drug regimen is instated by his doctor (on his wife's advice) to allow him to avoid all but the most severe of heart problems his genetic history says he might have. Jack's doctors tell him he is in the preventative phase of treatment for his as yet non-existent heart condition, and Jack complies. His weight falls as the new drug, diet and exercise regimen take effect, and he feels better. On his doctor's advice, Jack increases his payments to his life-enhancement policy to compensate for the eventuality that he'll have to have his heart repaired or replaced, and gets on with his day, which goes well until he sees the invoice from Maeve's gamete market transaction. Then his blood pressure hits the roof and he calls Maeve to scream at her down the phone line and change that *in utero* avatar that keeps appearing on his screen when she calls him. She hangs up on him after two seconds. Jack stares at the phone, fuming.

FACTOID: Vehicles powered only by electric motors have existed for almost as long as those powered by internal combustion engines. They have always been limited by the range on a single battery charge, but advances in battery technology, and the increasing cost and environmental impact of fossil fuels, could make electric cars competitive. Innovations which allow electric cars to be charged up at home overnight or to have their batteries exchanged should also help them to become accepted. Manufacturers are striving to bring electric cars to market, but they will face tough competition from improved internal-combustion-engine cars, hybrids, and fuel-cell cars.

9

Health

How much would you pay to live an extra ten years in good health? If the technology existed to allow this, would you purchase this technology now, or save up for it through a life-extension policy, much like life assurance is bought today? Would you even want such a thing? Whatever age you are now, ask yourself how much you'd pay for those extra years. Now write it down. You probably wrote down a number between €500,000 and €1 million.

In 2050, thanks to inflation, and despite the creep of ever-cheaper technology, that's a good estimate of what it will cost to get those ten years of rude and ruddy health. We are already seeing people born in the 1900s living to be 110 years old or more. These people are rare, but their numbers are growing[1]. Remember that the world's oldest lady, Edna Parker, was born in 1893, and lived through what history has come to call 'the extreme century'.

The twentieth century Edna saw come and go was a hard time to live in, and she did not have the medical, dietary and societal enhancements our children will come to expect. Yet she lived to be 115. The children of twenty-first-century Ireland have accidents, road deaths, pollution and climate change as the biggest external threats to their health. Though childhood obesity will damage the futures of many young people in Ireland in the next two generations, these children can expect to live long and fruitful lives, thanks to healthy diets, comfortable working conditions, and modern medicine. When they reach middle and old age, their lives will be prolonged by modern precision medicine. A more productive workforce will be able to retire later, and predictive and preventative medicines will be able to be developed via analysis of the genomic properties of illness.

In the first chapter of this book, I wrote that I was more interested in people than in technology, more interested in the societal effects of climate change, urbanisation, globalisation, and so forth, than the great advances in technology we will see in the next forty years. So I made a choice to stay away, as far as possible, from writing about robot monkey butlers, personal helicopters and cars that talk to you. In discussing health, however, it would be wrong to omit the beneficial effects of technology on health care outcomes. Trillions of euros are being directed into health-related research in areas such as biopharmacology and nanotechnology. These new technologies will change the face of medicine, and so I'm including a short description of some medical technologies here.

By 2050, medicine will have undergone a paradigm shift. Therapies aimed at preventing illness at the genetic level will probably be in widespread use, as will technologies to predict disease and modify our lifestyles accordingly. Medicine will be strongly focused on these preventative measures, in contrast to the current approach, where disease is dealt with on a macroscopic level if and when it presents itself. The latter requires more procedures and hospital time, and expensive and prolonged courses of medications, while the former, while costly to implement, could enable us to avoid many of the current costs of health care.

The idea of a specifically tailored diet and exercise regimen for someone whose genetic makeup suggests a likelihood of heart problems will remove the need for expensive heart-recuperation therapies such as heart transplants and keyhole surgeries to widen (or 'stent') clogged arteries.

Today's medicine is highly effective, but it is a blanket approach: when you find cancer, irradiate the system, and so forth. The current approach focuses on putting out fires, rather than preventing them starting and taking hold. In the case of cancer, this generalised approach is only 40 to 50 percent effective, meaning that only half of people who are given any treatment survive; and of course the treatments themselves often produce serious side effects. More than 100,000 people die each year in the US from the side effects of drugs, and another 2 million become seriously ill due to complications. There is another way.

Medicine is poised to enter a new era of personalised genomics. For those who can afford these new therapies, lifestyles – and life-spans – will be altered. For those who can't afford this technology, life-spans will be shorter. You can change your life right now by changing your diet and lifestyle, because what you eat, how you respond to emotional stress, whether or not you smoke cigarettes, how much you exercise, and how you experience love and intimacy all affect your health, either positively or negatively. Another way to change your health is to make new genes.

The complexity of genomic sequencing is staggering. In the case of, say, drug development, minute genetic differences must be identified and related causally to specific outcomes using a wide range of drugs. Many genes can influence a specific bodily function, and all these interactions must also be mapped out. And with 3 billion bits of information in our DNA, errors in coding may occur. Scientists can already manipulate genes to affect bodily functions. Most diseases, like cancer, begin at the atomic level, where subtle interactions between DNA and our genes, and the environment, as well as other parts of the body and – some think – the mind, interact.

The medicine of 2009 does not fully see, nor does it understand these interactions, but we know they exist. Once we can observe and understand the interactions, we can begin to think about changing them for the better. The cells in your body are tiny. Your body is made up of 100 trillion of them, and they operate on a miniature scale. By the time disease is at the level where you can perceive it with your senses, it is already well developed. By the time you feel that lump in your breast, or experience pain, or just feel 'wrong' about some part of your body or mind, the disease is well advanced and potentially very dangerous. If we could turn off the potential triggers of the disease with a vaccine, or carefully mould human behaviour through diet and exercise to avoid these outcomes, we would save millions of lives, and trillions of euro which is now spent fighting diseases of all kinds.

Several technologies have yet to be developed before this personalised medicine becomes reality. First, predictive genomics and nanotechnology will have to mesh with information technology and neuroscience to enhance the genetic makeup of the average human being. Again, the idea is to get an Irish person born in the next century to have the same level of fitness and health care outcomes as a person who is sixty years of age does now. The new medicine will be predictive and preventative, in that a blood test will scan for genomic deficiencies (like heart complaints), and therapies will be prescribed to prevent these deficiencies from ever occurring. The new medicine will allow the restoration or replacement of previously lost bodily functions like memories, sight or hearing, through robotics, human enhancements or newly grown organs. This is not so far-fetched: already, cochlear implants can help the deaf to hear, skin and bone are grown routinely, jaws and other facial features can be replaced or modified, and animal organs can be grown in research facilities. Humanised organs can now be grown inside animals, bringing a host of ethical issues into play[2].

MEDICAL INNOVATION: CAUSES AND CONSEQUENCES

What are the consequences for Irish society and the Irish economy of a vast array of medical technologies improving the lives and longevity or you and me – the adults of today – as well as our children and grandchildren? The extension of life for older people must be coupled with the extension of work practices, so that it won't be uncommon to see a man working well into his nineties. The consequences of a vastly more experienced workforce, as well as the depopulation caused by much lower birth rates in the generations which follow ours, will be a matter of the highest social importance[3].

Think about today's average Irish person, born in 1960, say, and their sense of social entitlement. As they grow up, their parents, and society, pay for their education. They go out into the workforce in their twenties, and pay taxes. In their late twenties to mid-thirties, they start a family and have two to three children. Their incomes go up as they become more productive and more experienced, and they pay more taxes, consume more, and make bigger decisions, like purchasing property. They work until they are sixty to sixty-five, and then retire, living another twenty to thirty years, until they die, most likely from cancer or an immuno-logical or heart-related illness[4].

There is a societal model to cope with this life cycle as it plays out again and again in Irish society. We are educated as children, we work as adults, we have children, our children have children, we retire, we die. Our children pay for us, as we have paid for them. Society replaces itself, as individual members come and go. This model is about to break down.

In an age of longer-living, more productive, but also less *re*productive Irish people, the sense that a person will have just one career will go out of the window – along with the notion of retiring at sixty-five. People who live to 125 or even 150 might have several partners, several jobs, and even several lives. Their existence will change the social model, because, essentially, by living longer, they are breaking the social contract I've just described. Demographically speak-ing, they are cheating[5]. You will be cheating, because, if you are old enough to read this book, you are very likely to live into your nineties or even later, if you look after yourself properly. And that is without the medical enhancements we will witness over the next forty years. There will not be enough people in the generation behind you to support a pension system that guarantees an income to someone for, perhaps, the last three decades of their life beyond retire-ment. The system will strain, creak, and eventually break, because what we're really talking about is a transfer of income, every year, from young people to old people[6].

Let's think about that.

Say you are thirty years old, and earn €50,000 a year. You pay, say, €10,000 a year in tax to the government. In that same year, the government has to fund the pension of someone who has stopped working, so it has to transfer all of that €10,000 to the pensioner. Two more people like you are required, in that year, to fund one pensioner on a pension of, say, €30,000. As the number of active workers stays much the same, but the number of pensioners explodes, thanks to the increased longevity of the population, governments will be hard pressed to fund anything other than pensions and health care. Expect a gradual clawback of services, with the attendant public outcry, by the early 2020s. The pensionable age will also creep, hop, and then jump up as the scale of the problem gets larger. And the situation will get worse. The projections are that public spending on pensions, health and long-term care is set to increase from 11 percent of Ireland's output in 2005 to some 21 percent in 2050. However, the upside of people living longer is that they will work for longer periods, learn more, earn more, and pay more taxes.

> *FACTOID:* The number of Americans who are exploring the concept of better living through antidepressant chemistry nearly doubled in the decade from 1996 to 2005 – and that was before the economic meltdown. Among users of antidepressants, the percentage receiving psychotherapy fell from 31.5 percent to less than 20 percent. About 80 percent of patients were treated by doctors other than psychiatrists[7].

HEALTH AND WEALTH

As we discussed in Chapter 2, one of the key ingredients of the explosive economic growth we witnessed during the

Celtic Tiger period in Ireland was an increase in participation in the labour market by women. In the coming decades, expect to see an increase in labour-market participation among older workers in more knowledge-intensive industries. The explosion in global economic productivity in recent years has been driven as much by fostering human resources – particularly through improvements in health, education and employment opportunities for women and girls – as by technological advances. As Ireland competes in an international set of knowledge-intensive markets, the skills and experience of (as well as the tax revenue from) older workers will count for more. Once these workers have finished having their children – in other words, by the time they are into their fifties – we may also see a second productivity bulge in certain sectors, as these people begin second (or third) careers, and contribute to the Irish economy for years to come; this may wipe out some, if not *all*, of the government's funding problems.

The reason not all of the government's funding problems will be wiped out is the type of work that these older workers will probably be engaged in. As we, and our children, age, the proportion of workers in the Irish economy who simply process facts on computers – knowledge workers – will increase. Knowledge work as a type of work to do is interesting, because one does not need to be 100 percent physically fit to do it well (trust me, I haven't been inside a gym this year), and the more often you do it, the better you become at it. Information, facts, and flows of facts will be freely and widely available in 2050; good judgement to interpret and understand the complex interactions around these facts will not. Experience is a scarce thing, and what is scarce has value – by which I mean that it commands a price. It will pay older workers to stay in the workforce, and so they shall. These workers will use the longevity-enhancing products to extend their time in the labour force, and, in parts, the Irish economy will be better off as a result.

WHERE WILL ALL THESE MIRACLE PRODUCTS BE COMING FROM IN THE FIRST PLACE?

The 76 million people born in the US between 1946 and 1964, called the 'baby boomers', redefined Western culture as they came of age, took power, changed the world, and now move into retirement and old age – having amassed large amounts of wealth, which they will now spend to remain healthy, active and alive. This investment capital, and the guaranteed market for products produced to service this demand, will be the spurs which kick the research and development of these technologies forward at a faster pace than other research and development initiatives[8]. The nano-, bio- and pharma-industries will supply products to meet this demand, and they will do it for a price. But the price for the *companies* will be less and less. Personalised medicine could improve drug development by guiding more precise trials using a few hundred patients instead of three thousand to five thousand. What will the cost be? The price of the insurance policy I asked you to consider at the start of this chapter, at least.

It is important to realise that for-profit product innovation occurs first at the behest of the rich. As we saw in Chapter 8, Ireland will contain many more rich people by 2050. We will be a nation of investors, innovators and instigators, who direct capital into investments we think will achieve higher levels of remuneration. The drugs and therapies developed over the next forty years will be developed by the rich, and for the rich. Unfortunately, the poor won't have much of a look-in though, over time, they will gain access to these therapies as they become cheaper. Research and development of medicines for the privileged will mean an increase in inequality in Ireland, as those who are unable to afford longevity-enhancing therapies and restorative medicines privately will be forced to wait for these technologies – or perhaps not access them at all.

Changes in health care provision will affect us individually, socially, and culturally. Expect legal battles as older, healthier people vie – and lobby – for the rights to public provision of enhancements and life-prolonging medical treatments from a government which is increasingly constrained by mounting expenditure on pensions and health care. We are currently witnessing a fight for the rights of children and the disabled in Ireland. Senior citizens will be next to have their voices heard and their concerns addressed. Individually, where you stand in the distribution of income will determine how long you will live, because how much you save through your pension contributions, and health insurance, life assurance, and life enhancement policies, will broadly determine the length of your life. The world of work will change, as older workers become an increasingly significant part of the labour market. You and I will work into our seventies and eighties, and our children will work at least a decade longer. Vast and varied experience will change the workplace and the markets, as more products are targeted towards wealthy, older and more active consumers.

The ethical issues raised by the implementation of these new technologies will change Irish society[9].

To take one example: in 2006, Adriana Iliescua, a

sixty-five-year-old woman, gave birth to a healthy baby girl via in vitro fertilisation, and a donor egg. Despite the risks to herself and her daughter, Iliescua's one regret was that she did not look like a younger woman for her daughter. She said: 'I am always amazed when I look in the mirror and see myself. There is such a difference between what I feel and what I see.' Whatever your opinion of the ability of a woman in her sixties to give birth, women like Iliescua will continue to want children, and modern science will provide them. As the debates over stem-cell usage, human cloning, and animal rights rage on into the middle of the twenty-first century, we should expect to see scientific developments creating more ethical dilemmas than it solves.

FACTOID: Genetic therapy may represent the Holy Grail of medicine because so much illness is inherited from the approximately five thousand genetic disorders that have been identified. The decoding of the human genome has not reached the point where genetic blue-prints have been mapped for all these diseases, and the techniques for altering genetic traits remain crude. A defective gene was corrected in a patient for the first time in 2009. Researchers at the Salk Institute used cell-programming techniques to convert the patient's cells into stem cells and used a virus to transport them into the body. This breakthrough is considered to mark the beginning of a new age of curative treatments. Today, more than three hundred companies are developing genetic therapies involving eight hundred clinical trials.

MEDICAL TOURISM AND THE IRISH HEALTH SERVICE

Irish people have always travelled abroad, since the island was first settled around eight thousand years ago. In the modern era of mass international travel, medical tourism is likely to become both more and less common. Let me explain. Currently, it is possible to have your teeth seen to by Bulgarian dentists in specialised dental clinics near the airports around Sofia, Plovdiv and Varna. The most extreme cases go to the US, and when waiting lists get too long, patients are sent to the UK for certain surgeries. For those who want them, abortions are carried out in the UK. These are examples of specialised and well-defined medical procedures being performed on Irish people abroad. In the case of the dentist, cost is the driving factor. For those travelling to the UK for surgeries to bring down waiting lists, the health implications of waiting, and the systemic failure of our health service, are the driving factors. For those choosing to abort their foetuses, the driving factor is a complex interplay of ethical, social and cultural factors.

In 2050, Irish people will routinely travel abroad to seek the best medical procedures. Our sunnier summers, discussed in Chapter 5, combined with Irish medical expertise, may also bring medical tourists here. Those who can afford it will travel anywhere in the world to receive the highest-quality treatment, or to save money on what will be standard procedures and enhancements. Medical tourism will boom as an industry in the era of personalised medicine. Other, less skills-intensive medical procedures will be carried out in Ireland at drop-in clinics and supermarkets. Only the poorest and most urgent cases will go to hospitals and through the public health system. These institutions will see their resources cut in real terms as the scale of the Irish government's fiscal crisis becomes more apparent.

HSE 2.0

The current Irish health service is a creation of Victorian-era social thinking[10]. The organised provision of health services to the public by concerned doctors, concerned citizens, and philanthropists occurred in the early 1700s, with Ireland's first public hospital opening its doors in the 1720s. The Catholic Church maintained a presence in community-based health care through the nineteenth century, and in the mid-nineteenth century the British government instituted the workhouse system, which provided medical officers, infirmaries and dispensaries to the poor.

In 1947, following on from the influential Beveridge Report of 1942, a national health system for Ireland was instated. This rapidly became a complicated two-tier system, where private patients skipped the long queues created by those paid for by the public purse – that is, unless they didn't, for a variety of reasons. The administrative system created in the 1950s was revamped in the 1970s with the introduction of the medical card and the creation of eight health boards, and was revamped again in 2004 with the merging of the eleven health boards into one Health Service Executive (HSE).

The HSE as it exists in 2009 has many problems. First, the provision of health services is highly uneven, depending on where you happen to be in the country. The closure of many regional services has caused anger among local communities, who see their sickest being forced to commute in order to access much-needed care. Recent expressions of public anger over the closure or reduction of services have contributed to a feeling of crisis within the HSE. The HSE argues in its defence that health care spending by the government has never been higher. This is true: over the last ten years, spending by the government on health has tripled. Health outcomes have not improved in parallel, however, and critics say that many of the increases in government spending have gone on salary payments and capital improvements rather than on increased service provision.

Where does the HSE go from here? The next few years will see relatively few changes in the structure of the system. Yet over the next forty years, the structure of the system will have to change, because of the stresses which will be placed upon it by a population of more than 7 million people, many of whom will be older and will require at least some health care. In particular, the private-public mix of patients which currently exists will have to be abandoned. A health service which is free at the point of care for 100 percent of its citizens is not viable when the number of citizens living to older age increases, and costs of care increase in a boundless way. Those who can pay privately should seek care in privately run hospitals, with public patients seen by publicly funded medical professionals. Clinical care should take place at the community, rather than at the hospital level, but up to recently, regional and local clinics received only 16 percent of the total HSE budget, and so remain critically underfunded. Cost pressures will move many of the outpatient procedures which are normally found in hospitals to clinics and drop-in centres, while surgical provisions become increasingly centralised and specialised. The future history of the HSE will entail the adoption of another model of care for its patients, one where every category of illness which cannot be prevented or restored by modern medicine must be treated at home, in a private facility, abroad, or in a public hospital. The sad fact, I fear, is that rising inequality will contribute to those who are wealthy enough to be able to afford private care experiencing much more satisfactory health care outcomes, and therefore longer lives, simply because of their ability to pay.

The HSE will also perform another function, which, until recently, it has not had to deal with: infectious-disease control, as diseases which develop here in Ireland, and abroad, threaten public safety. In addition to the current AIDS pandemic, there is reason to worry about various other pandemics and global diseases. One of the most startling aspects of the twenty-first century will be the degree to which ordinary people remain connected to one another throughout their lives, via the internet and so-called 'social media'. Societies and economies are also becoming more connected, in a process called globalisation, which began in the Industrial Revolution and has waxed and waned throughout modern economic history. In terms of health, globalisation can increase the likelihood of our survival by connecting us to those health care professionals who are best equipped to help us. But increasing connectivity between regions also allows germs and pathogens to travel to new sites – including those that are not prepared for them.

The first global pandemic of the twenty-first century will most likely be imported from Africa, and may be one of the virulent strains of Lassa fever, Rift Valley fever, Marburg virus, Ebola virus, or Bolivian hemorrhagic fever. Antibiotic-resistant microorganisms like MRSA, which grow in hospitals, or a new, highly contagious form of atypical pneumonia such as SARS, and even less virulent but equally contagious forms of influenza, like human swine flu, might also be possible candidates for a global pandemic.

What is certain is the influence that global connectivity will have on the transmission of highly infectious diseases. New airport scanners, hygiene protocols, and disease-control surfaces at transport hubs like airports may help to contain the problem, but with a sufficiently virulent strain, the outcome for Irish citizens may not be good.

Another, more serious problem is international patient record-keeping. Different countries keep different levels of information about their citizens, and most of that information is kept on paper. The US medical system is one of the most advanced medical systems on the planet. Electronic medical records are in the forefront of IT adoption, yet only 17 percent of US physicians use them. Addressing the lack of transferrable patient information will be crucial in the new markets for health.

In the next chapter, we'll explore how educational and health-related inequalities will give rise to an extremely unequal Ireland in 2050.

HAPPINESS IS . . .

13 August 2050

Maeve isn't happy, as her invoice has come in from the company managing her gamete market transaction. Maeve feels that she's been overcharged. Maeve asked for a gamete match from a father with a strong heart, to counter her own father's heart problems, and this genomic modification wasn't cheap. Scans of the baby indicated that a simple genetic modification would do the trick. She also asked for her child to have blue eyes and black hair, have the potential to reach six foot two, and be well above average in intelligence. All of this cost a lot more than her father had anticipated. Because she bought on the open market from a vendor in India (on her father's recommendation), exchange-rate movements over the last few months have increased the price of her gamete match. She's fairly sure that her father would kill her if she wasn't pregnant with such an expensive baby.

Maeve gets a text from her onetime boyfriend Patrick: does she want to meet?

IS THIS ALL THERE IS?

1 September 2050

A young man, dressed in workman's clothes, stands at the door of an overcrowded Accident and Emergency department in Dublin. His head is bleeding from a cut he received at work. He can't find a place to sit, so he leans against the wall. He is seen by Nurse Sarah Hayes after an hour. Standing at the door, Sarah cleans his cut, gives him two painkillers and a small bandage, and sends him on his way. He marches out holding the bandage to his head, asking loudly: 'Is this all you get for the taxes you pay?' The door hits him on the way out. The door apologises in a calm and pleasing female voice.

FACTOID: We are replaceable. An astonishing array of body parts can now be replaced with artificial equivalents: skin, bone, blood vessels, cochlea, heart valves, pacemakers, knees, hips and so on. 'Name almost any human disability,' wrote *BusinessWeek*, 'and there's probably research under way to overcome it.' Experts forecast that a good artificial heart will be developed by 2010, lung and kidneys by 2015, brain cells by 2017, muscles by 2019, eyes by 2024, and the brain itself by 2035. Some devices, such as joint replacements, pacemakers and heart valves, have long-term reliability. Americans replaced 383,000 hip joints – and 555,000 knees – with metal implants during 2005, and, across the globe, more than 190,000 people have electrodes in their heads to control the tremors associated with Parkinson's disease. Seventy thousand Americans have artificial cochleas to restore hearing.

10

INEQUALITY AND EXCLUSION: HOMELESS IN DUBLIN IN 2050?

> The growing affluence, the new technologies, the great shift in personal relations . . . and above all the revolution in the Catholic Church which made provisional much that appeared timeless and changeless – all this produced something of a state of anomie: that lonely, anxious state where men no longer look to the warmth of fellowship, but seek all the time to acquire goods, to compete for success, to appear dominant since they have no other means of winning the regard of others and consequently of achieving self-regard; and an envy that is so naked as to be disreputable.[1]

This quote, excoriating the materialistic Irish culture of greed and envy, could have been written about the Celtic Tiger period of the 1990s. It wasn't. The writer Charles McCarthy wrote this paragraph about the Ireland of the 1960s.

Ireland today is a pretty unequal place[2]. Looking around

you every day, you see examples of groups of people enjoying lives which are vastly different from those of their neighbours. The children of the rich enjoy opportunities and resources far in advance of those of the children of the poor, and the use of those opportunities and resources compounds the difference between rich and poor children throughout their lives. Recent studies[3] have found that 50 percent of the variance in inequality in lifetime earnings is determined by the age of eighteen. The family plays a powerful role in shaping adult outcomes – a role that is is not fully recognised at many levels in Ireland. In this chapter, we will look at how the confluence of health, wealth, age and what I'll call 'digital inequality' will continue to cause a rift in Irish society which will resonate through the next forty years.

WHY DOES INEQUALITY MATTER?

It has been known for many years that poor health and violence are much more prevalent in unequal societies than in more equal ones[4]. These problems are not related to average incomes; in other words, if you made everyone in a society twice as rich, you wouldn't change the situation. The finding holds for many countries, and throughout the fifty US states. The impact of inequality is particularly severe for children: the more unequal a society, the more the well-being of children is negatively affected. The focus of this research is not always income inequality (how many multiples of my salary yours is); rather, researchers think of income inequality as measuring in some sense the distance between classes of people, and perhaps even the degree of social stratification a society experiences. More unequal societies, like Ireland and the United States, have, on average, a lower quality of life than more equal societies. Recent research has pointed out that the life-diminishing results of valuing economic growth above equality in rich societies causes people's lives to be shorter, unhealthier and unhappier. Inequality in a society increases the rate of teenage pregnancy, violence, obesity, imprisonment and addiction; it destroys relationships between individuals born in the same society but into different classes. Inequality also works as a driver of consumption through the 'keeping up with the Joneses' effect, and so helps to deplete the planet's resources.

To take one example which is very well studied, America is one of the world's richest nations, with one of the highest levels of income per person of any modern society, but Americans have the lowest life expectancy of the developed nations, and there is an extremely high level of violence, in particular murder, in American society. Of all crimes, those involving violence are most closely related to high levels of inequality, and this finding is consistent within a country, within a state, and even within a particular city. For some, mainly young, men with no economic or educational route to achieving the high status and earnings required for full citizenship, the experience of daily life at the bottom of a steep social hierarchy is enraging. Inequality affects mental health as well: around a quarter of British people, and more than a quarter of Americans, experience mental-health problems in any given year, compared with fewer than 10 percent of the population in Japan, Germany, Sweden and Italy[5].

Some people are richer than others in Ireland; on the face of it, I don't think this is necessarily a bad thing. It's just life. Some people work harder, some people are smarter, still more people are just born lucky – either with natural abilities (sporting ones, say) or different resources (being born rich). Realistically, we can't change these facts. What matters more is equality of opportunity, and reducing overall poverty and social exclusion. Will Ireland in 2050 produce these types of outcomes for its weaker members? Will we still see homelessness on the streets of our major cities?

THE RISE OF THE MIDDLE CLASS

What does it mean to be middle class? It means to own a decent-size home, to have a regular income, to have consumer freedom. Today in Ireland, being middle class probably means that you drive a gas-burning vehicle and, in general, consume heavily. And when people consume, they consume oil. As Chapter 5 showed, the more people who consume fossil fuels, the more likely it is that environmental degradation will occur. Also, as the population grows (and becomes richer), and more people become middle class, the effects of middle-class levels of consumption will be felt across Irish society and through our environment.

There has always been a substantial middle class in Ireland, but it rose to prominence as a political and cultural force in the 1950s and 1960s. Together with agricultural interests, this class has been the main driver of political and social power since then: every political party has shaped its policies to find favour with these two groups. The middle classes throughout history have, at different times and to differing degrees, championed freedom of conscience, human rights, privacy, property rights, reason and science[6]. In Ireland, the middle classes are a force for stability and conservatism and, whether you like it or not, their ranks are growing.

We have seen that economic growth in Ireland may be hindered by the twin problems of an ageing society and climate change, and that these phenomena will impose significant costs on Irish society, but we can still expect that, by 2050, our grandchildren will be at least twice as wealthy as we are now. Because of a larger, richer population, more people will be middle class, and there will be more of them. As the middle classes get larger, those who were previously poor will be drawn into their ranks – which is a very good thing for those people, because individually their standards of living will rise.

We can see the effects of a larger middle class in Irish society today, in part. Thanks to the last fifteen years of economic growth, there is now a large (and growing) lower-middle class in Ireland, many of them home-owners, parents, entrepreneurs and investors.

There are many benefits to being middle class. For example, the children of the middle classes tend to be more educated, and go on to experience longer lives, lived at higher levels of income, than the children of the poor. They also tend to be slimmer: though childhood obesity is a problem for many Irish parents, it is far more prevalent among people from lower-income households. So while the future is not all rosy for the middle classes, being middle class is certainly better than being poor.

WHO ARE THE POOR IN 2050?

One of the functions of any state is to redistribute wealth away from those who have it towards those who do not. A large part of the Irish government's mission is to reduce the numbers of people living in relative poverty – that is, the number of people who have to live with less than would be socially acceptable generally[7]. (There are problems with measuring poverty in this way, because if you decide that I am poor because I am half as wealthy as the average person, and both our incomes double, then I am still poor, by your definition[8] – but I digress.)

I think it is better to think that poverty means not being *capable* of living a minimally 'normal' life, where by 'normal' I mean being able to live without shame, to visit and entertain your friends, to keep track of what's going on in the world, and perhaps to exercise some of your wants or to pursue some of your goals in life. If I increased your income and your resources (giving you food, clothing, shelter, an iPod, sunglasses, and so on), I could move you out of poverty by giving you the capability to visit your friends (perhaps you'd wear those sunglasses I just gave you), and to pursue your goals in life.

Even if living standards were to double in Ireland in the next two generations, sadly there will still be those who experience poverty as I've defined it; they will experience poverty mainly because they have no job. The lack of access to money and resources, as well as the removing of personal contacts and social networks, means that not having a job is a hardship for many people in Irish society. They must support themselves through social welfare payments, savings (such as pensions or retirement accounts) or unearned income from their families.

Another issue to be considered when it comes to thinking about those people who are incapable (as I've defined it) of living a 'normal' life is to see their problem in the light of the lack of support they get from not being able to make choices for themselves in many situations. There are three classes of people who are most likely to have this problem: the young, the old, and the ill or disabled. To answer the question of this section, they are still the poor, as I see it, in

2050. Even more alarming, most research done on the subject shows that children who experience poverty tend to go on to experience it as adults; this implies that poverty will continue in Ireland into the twenty-second century. A 2005 study found that almost 27 percent of people aged twenty-five to sixty-five who experienced financial difficulties 'most of the time or often' in their household as teenagers were at risk of poverty as adults[9]. The comparable figure for respondents[10] who 'never' experienced financial difficulties as teenagers was much lower, at 11 percent.

We can change things, and help alleviate this state of affairs. Policies aimed at helping underprivileged youths in Ireland would, if successful, set off a stream of benefits into the future if it returned them to education, or helped them get a job. The notion of child poverty is particularly troubling when we consider how it has the ability to affect our society for decades into the future. Child poverty, besides being morally offensive to most people, is linked to a host of social problems which affect not only those who experience poverty, but also those around them: their neighbours and neighbourhoods.

A stitch in time saves nine. A policy directed towards increasing community connections between middle-class and poverty-stricken areas would help alleviate widespread social isolation, which I view as a major threat to a well-functioning Ireland in 2050. I touched on this theme in the last chapter, but it is worth repeating that in our new suburbs, people might know only six to ten other people in their locality, and these would most likely be family members.

In large-scale regeneration programmes like the one we have in Limerick, quality new homes and a new social landscape, together with improved community services, are designed to increase social inclusion – at massive public expense. Coupled with smaller, locally organised (and locally funded) community initiatives, these community-enhancing endeavours can go a long way towards reducing social problems like social isolation and disaffection. In working to reduce poverty, we will also be taking steps to reduce the level of social isolation many people will experience in years to come.

HOMELESS IN DUBLIN?

Homelessness is perhaps the most extreme form of social exclusion. People who are homeless experience much higher levels of Hepatitis C, HIV, TB, poor nutrition, drug and alcohol addiction, and mental-health difficulties than people who have homes[11]. A society that solves the problem of homelessness will go a long way towards making itself a very nice place to live, because along the way to the solution of homelessness, many other problems associated with it will have to be solved. For example, it is known that the likelihood of someone ending up homeless is linked to whether they have a mental illness or not. Helping to understand the ways in which someone with a mental illness may become homeless also helps us to care for those with mental illnesses more effectively.

When I talk about ending homelessness, I mean that no one should have to sleep outside if they don't want to. If they have an emergency, they should be taken care of, and once that emergency has passed, they should not be let drift into a cycle of temporary or sheltered accommodation, bed-and-breakfast accommodation, and the street.

Many of the most vulnerable people in Ireland will come from the three categories I described above: the elderly (that's you and me in 2050, remember), the ill or disabled, and the young. Homelessness is often immediately preceded by a crisis in an individual's life. There are many triggers for homelessness, including the point when a relationship breaks down, when someone is evicted, or when they leave hospital, prison or state care. These individuals may fall through the cracks in the system, especially if there are not appropriate facilities for their care after, say, a spell in a hospital. The stories repeat themselves; they also point to a structural problem, which is that, given that there are channels through which homelessness occurs, surely it makes sense to think about how these channels might be closed off in the future?

As Irish society ages, increasing numbers of older people will put pressure on a variety of services. Older people are much more likely to live alone than younger people, but they need additional care as they do so. This will mean that additional sheltered housing and residential care will be needed to help older people in the future. It is important to stress that an ageing population does not necessarily have a direct impact on homelessness. It is possible that, with an increasing number of people over seventy, there will be a growing number of single older people living in substandard accommodation (because they cannot afford to repair their homes), and with a growing range of support needs. However, these people will probably not be classified by the state as homeless, but rather as elderly. The real reason why an ageing population is important to people working with the homeless is that it will absorb large amounts of energy, capital and resources from the housing and social-services sectors. An ageing population will also compete for political will and financial capital, as well as for skilled and committed staff, and people's charitable donations[12].

Sad to say, I'm sceptical as to whether we can eliminate

homelessness from Ireland in the next forty years. I see local authorities as the key to solving the problem, liaising with volunteer groups to secure single-person rented accommodation from the private sector at a reasonable rate. Simple assessment criteria for the needs of the homeless are not in place, and given the competition for resources I alluded to above, I simply don't see these groups tackling poverty (which causes homelessness), and homelessness itself in a significant way in the medium term. So we will still see homeless people on the streets of Dublin in forty years' time.

FACTOID: As markets become global and the traditional workplace gives way to cyberspace as the place to do business, only the elite will have anything to offer to the world's economies. There is solid evidence that the ups and downs in wage inequality across the twentieth century can be explained by a race between educational attainment and technological change. Technological change increases the demand for skilled workers, who are 'created' by better educational systems. It turns out that changes in the pace of educational attainment, rather than changes in technological progress, supply most of the facts of the story. The rise – and decline – of unions plays a supporting role in the story, as of course do migration and outsourcing. But not much of a role. Stripped to its essentials, the ebb and flow of wage inequality is all about education and technology.

DIGITAL INEQUALITY

Chapter 3 pointed to the need for digital literacy in addition to basic literacy, in today's Ireland, for everyone. As more key services like banking, taxation and local government move online, those who choose not to make the move online will be caught in a particularly problematic area: they will be on the wrong side of a digital divide. As better-paying jobs, and more opportunities in general, will exist online, those without the skills to take advantage of these opportunities will lose out, as will their children. It is likely that almost every middle-class child will have access to the internet in school or at home in the twenty-first century, but those who do not will be placed at a significant disadvantage.

HEALTH INEQUALITY

Chapter 9 described a near-utopia of genetically specific tests, giving health care professionals the ability to prescribe preventative life plans for the majority of Irish citizens. Irish health services have moved away from a model of attempting to provide universal health care at similar levels of quality to all patients to a public/private mix, where a queue exists for almost every health care resource, such as doctors, nurses and physiotherapists, along with all the machinery, imaging apparatus and diagnostic equipment they now need to do their jobs. Private patients can skip parts of the queue in places, and avail of specialist expertise, improved hospital conditions, and elective procedures. For those who can afford the new genomic tests, their health will be extended as a result of their wealth. For those who cannot, the alternative will be a high-quality public service that will offer the basics: a stripped-down, more efficient version of the health service we have today. Private hospitals and private doctors will actively 'cherry-pick' patients to reduce the likelihood of any adverse problems, while the public services will be burdened with the worst cases. This type of separation, and health inequality, is a policy choice we seem to be making as a nation in the twenty-first century.

Ireland is currently an unequal place to live, and I think that, into the middle of this century, it will become more, rather than less, unequal, with all the negative effects that rising inequality brings. The negative effects of increased inequality are decreased trust between people, lower standards of living for those at the bottom of the pile, strange changes to the composition of Irish society (especially through immigration), and in particular, changes in community life and social relations. I'm not a socialist. In fact, I'd like to see the market enter into as many areas of life as possible, though I recognise that there are limits to markets and their usefulness. My personal opinions, however, don't change the data researchers uncover when they look at the differences between societies: those societies that are more equal get that way by taking more from the rich, and giving more to the poor, using the government as a redistributive mechanism for doing so. People in more egalitarian countries live well, enjoy high living standards, and have excellent social conditions. I think that Ireland will not choose to reduce inequality by increasing taxes on the wealthy and increasing public service provision, because we have never done so in the past. Irish people have consistently voted into power governments that promise to keep taxes low. When taxes are low and economic growth is not in double digits, public services like education and health suffer. Richer elements in society do, have, and will prosper, because they can afford to secure private provision of these services. As the gap between private and public health widens due to medical innovation, and the digital divide effectively bars poorer and less educated people from the best jobs, inequality in Ireland will, sadly, grow. In short, we will see homelessness and continued general social exclusion in Ireland in the next forty years.

In the next chapter, we'll look at one of the most important drivers in Irish society: our government. The government of Ireland wields power over us, its citizens. Or does it?

A NEW ARRIVAL

1 and 2 September 2050

Although she can feel smaller contractions at 10 PM, Maeve goes into labour at 1 AM on 2 September 2050. The well-rehearsed birthing plan promptly goes out the window. Heavy rains have kept Maeve's boyfriend Patrick from getting to the Murphys' home, and Maeve is upset and scared. Sarah and a midwife are on hand to reassure her, and Jack and Bobby are on standby. Jim has left word that he is to be woken when the new arrival is with them.

A screen flickers, and it's Patrick. Maeve asks him where he is, and he tells her that he'll make it when the rain stops, but that he'll be there for her on the screen. Maeve asks for her dad. Jack holds her hand as her daughter, Emily, is born.

Jack is the first to hold her. It is 4.30 AM. Both mother and daughter are fine. Sarah cautions everyone on pain of death not to call her 'granny'.

11

Our Government: National, Regional and Local

Ireland's government is a complex, complicated organisation which reaches into our lives on a daily basis. The state educates us, it provides a health service for us, and it administers justice on our behalf (or, if we transgress, it administers justice upon us). The state takes taxes and spends those taxes on education, health and social welfare, as well as a host of other, smaller projects and subsidies. It rewards through political patronage at the local level and punishes through reduced regional investment. The trend in global politics is towards carefully crafted political blandness, coupled with fast-approaching – and often completely unpredictable – outbursts of oddness, panic and scandal. Ireland's politics are no different. Crises tend to mould politicians, because the politicians have no choice other than to react to them. Emergencies like the current economic downturn tend to glue nations together into large-scale coalitions of the willing – the League of Nations (the precursor to the UN) after

World War I, the European Union after World War II, and so on. Two centuries of economic thought and industrial development have shown that there is no workable method by which a nation can prosper on its own. We must trade with each other, and organise as nations together, despite our differences.

Ireland's political parties themselves lack real political divisions. The distinctions in political philosophies between Fianna Fáil and, say, the Labour Party are really only cosmetic. Ideology is impractical and unwieldy when a party holds power, and is most often jettisoned in the act of using power because of the constraints now placed on the holders of power by recent history – whatever current crisis happens to be playing out at the time, and whatever the political culture of the day happens to be. The government really only has a few choices it can reasonably make, so it makes them, and the results of whatever action it has to take are later 'spun' to appease any critics – until the next news cycle or crisis starts.

The practice of government in the twenty-first century is a neutered thing, stripped of the charisma and allure which drew the would-be wielders of power to it in the first place. But this is no bad thing: governments now function much more efficiently because of it: removing the glamour of government ensures that the boring work of actually running a country can go on unimpeded. The public can rest assured that policy will be dictated and directed by those with absolutely no incentive to, or interest in, rocking the boat: civil servants, academics, and policy wonks. The provision of new and better banking laws, Customs and Excise regulations, business codes of conduct, accounting standards, hygiene practices, school curricula, and regulations on insider trading, amongst a thousand other functions, leave the government merely as a referee for lobbyist-laden interest groups and for-profit enterprises, while the actual work of the nation continues. What we see is an unmoving and inert utopia of bureaucratic tedium resting beneath a foaming, churning squall of interest-group politics packaged and resold by the media for public consumption and diversion[1].

The goal of most public servants is the maintenance of the status quo at minimal cost to themselves and their individual organisations. The goal is clear: no great leaps forward can be made, no grand vision can be enacted by a charismatic leader. The model to follow is that of the (relatively) stable, open capitalist state, which gives its citizens a high standard of living, low inflation, low tariffs, politically independent central banks, direct foreign ownership of capital assets, and privatisation of many previously public services, like telecommunications and some aspects of health care. The stable capitalist nation-state, by virtue of its stability, also removes the opportunities for atrocities, campaigning, marching, rioting or organising. In such a culture, voting becomes virtually meaningless as an activity, because each party is guaranteed to last a maximum of only five years in the case of Ireland. The feeling is best expressed by the sociologist C. Wright Mills[2]:

> Not wishing to be disturbed over moral issues of the political economy, Americans cling to the notion that the government is a sort of automatic machine, regulated by the balancing of competing interests.

This is the modern state as we experience it in Ireland: an automatic machine for the regulation and satisfaction of competing interests and the entertainment of the body public, resting atop a civil service and decision-making apparatus devoted almost entirely to the reproduction of predictable and manageable social outcomes.

No description of the Ireland of the future would be complete without discussing where I think the government of this country is headed, and where it might take us.

This chapter looks at the future of Irish government by, first, looking at where local government came from. We'll see that our local governments are products of their histories, and that the choices they can make in the future are bound by that history. We have already looked at strategic national priorities for the government in Chapter 1: in the coming decades, we should look to the West. This chapter is more concerned with the government as you experience it in your daily life: through local authorities, and in your interactions with An Garda Síochána, An Post, and all of the public-service apparatus built by the government to implement its designs. Now, before we begin talking about the role of government, let me say a little about what I think governments should do, and what they should do for us. While I'm a proponent of free markets for most things, I'm not of the view that they work well everywhere and always.

Where the market won't produce something the public would benefit from, the government has to step in; and to do so, the government needs to tax its citizens in order to be able to afford whatever 'stepping in' actually entails. For example, no firm is going to provide streetlights, because at the point of sale – when you are walking underneath the lights – the firm can't charge for them. Can you imagine being stopped and asked for money every time you passed under a streetlight? Streetlights are incredibly useful tools, so the government must buy them. To get the money to make the streetlight purchase (and, in fact, to manufacture them), the government will have to levy taxes on current incomes, mostly. The first part of this chapter's discussion about the government should then be framed in terms of taxation.

When you compare Ireland to other developed nations like the US, the UK, France, Germany and Italy, we in Ireland have had, on average, relatively low taxes since the formation of the state. The Irish people have consistently chosen lower taxes when they could, and political parties, in a completely rational effort to win power, have given lower taxes to the people. So, contrary to popular belief, we are a low-tax country. But without high levels of economic growth, low taxes mean that public services, which are paid for through taxes, will be provided only at low levels.

Ireland is now about to return to the level of income taxes seen in the mid-1990s. New taxes may be introduced – taxes on property, on carbon usage, on pensions – and old subsidies, which are reverse taxes, because they send government money towards firms, rather than collecting them, may be removed.

While taxes used to be very high in Ireland in the 1980s, this is no longer the case. Ireland scores fourth-lowest in Europe in terms of the share of total tax revenue as a percentage of total economic output. Ireland's share of total tax revenue as a percentage of total economic output was only 31 percent in 2003. This compares to 51 percent in Sweden, 49 percent in Denmark, 42 percent in the United Kingdom and 29.1 percent in Latvia. The notion that we have a high-tax economy should be dispelled.

The first step we need to take now as a country is to agree how much the government is going to take from its citizens in the form of taxation. Everything else flows from that choice. Assuming that Ireland retains an average taxation-to-overall-economic-output ratio of around 23 to 25 percent, and our population grows steadily – and we don't have another Celtic Tiger episode before 2050 – then Ireland can probably afford to spend something like €55 to €80 billion per year on public services. One important distinction needs to be made here between central taxation and other taxation, because increasing funding in percentage terms to local authorities, by allowing them to collect some kinds of tax, will change the political landscape in Ireland.

Central taxation is taxation revenue that goes straight into the Exchequer, not to local authorities or to other bodies. The local authorities in Ireland receive much of their operating funds from central government, creating an issue of local and regional power versus central big government. There is little real autonomy for the local authorities because of the funding structures in place. Looking at the top ten EU countries in terms of taxation, local and regional taxation makes up over 8 percent of the output of these countries. In Ireland, it makes up just 0.8 percent of overall output, accounting for a little over 2 percent of tax revenues. In fact, Ireland has one of the most centralised set of government services in Europe.

To conclude: we have poor public services, in large part, because we haven't funded them properly for long enough. The billions of euro spent on health, education and welfare during the Celtic Tiger years helped us catch up with other developed nations only partially. These countries had all developed steadily in the 1950s, 1960s and 1970s, as Ireland languished as an economic basket case, so it should not be surprising that its performance today is below par in many areas.

Think of the public services as a human body, with funding as the body's nutrition. You can't take a person for a month, feed them bread and water for twenty-five days, then switch to two steaks a day, and complain that the person is underweight and weak at the end of the thirty days. The total investment in Ireland's public services over a forty-year period has been much lower than that in other developed nations, because Ireland has not generated the kind of sustained growth necessary to develop these services to their fullest extent as modern entities.

Major investments are still required just to bring the health and education sectors up to the same level as their counterparts in other countries. These investments, largely, come from taxes. The government can raise taxes, which would be politically difficult, or it could decide to reduce the amount of public services made available overall, and streamline its offerings, knowing that increased public provision of services means that private provision won't become as well developed as it might have been, because businesses find it hard to compete with services given away for free by the government. As always in the public-private debate, those people who fall between the cracks will suffer[3], as we saw in Chapter 10.

THE END OF TRULY LOCAL GOVERNMENT

Local government in Ireland is a complex set of arrangements that evolved from a nineteenth-century British movement centred around government fulfilment of local needs and wants[4]. Our municipal local governments arose from the nineteenth-century statutes of the British Parliament enacted to meet several social needs. The Poor Relief (Ireland) Act of 1838, for example, gave powers and money to organisations (which would later become our local authorities) to feed and clothe the poor in each area. Interestingly, the most respected economists of their day, David Ricardo and Thomas Malthus, were vehemently opposed to any Poor Law in Ireland. They argued that any state-sponsored alms for Ireland's poor would only exacerbate Irish people's natural tendencies towards 'improvidence, idleness, pauperism and lack of enterprise'. The economists were voted down, but only because the general opinion in the ruling Whig party was that without a Poor Law, Ireland's paupers would board boats en masse for Blighty, determined to live out their lives on the backs of the hard-working ratepayers of England[5].

Local authorities were given their current status in the Local Government (Ireland) Act of 1898, and have since developed into modern arms of government, steadily extending their original remits of poor relief into public health and hygiene, waste disposal, housing, planning and development of urban and rural areas, keeping the peace and the administration of justice, civil registrations like births and deaths, the provision and running of public parks, graveyard maintenance, and a thousand other functions, including local taxation.

Of course, in addition to these functions, the secondary function of any local-governance structure is the returning of members of the right political persuasion to the Dáil. The local authorities are created to foster political patronage, as well as to agitate for more money and power at the local level. The second president of Sinn Féin, John Sweetman, was an early proponent of local councils and authorities gaining enough power to displace the national ruling body in its local area, essentially through one funding source: the rating system.

After 1900, local authorities gradually lost their power and functions with regard to poverty reduction as the state began actively pushing state-sanctioned social welfare policies. Many functions were transferred to a tightly centralised, modern state architecture. The future had arrived, and by the early 1930s, Ireland's cities were managed differently from rural areas, with professional managers for Dublin, Cork and Limerick being appointed. The final blow to the power of local authorities came in 1977, when the government of the day abolished taxes levied on water-usage rates[6]. Today, local authorities derive much of their income from motor-taxation collection and a 'rate support grant' paid by the central government to local authorities.

Because the local authorities are underfunded, they perform poorly, and because they perform poorly, proponents of a centrally controlled government use their underperformance as an argument for further reducing local authorities' funding, and with it their influence and power.

Why do local authorities matter so much in 2050? Today, most daily social services are, in fact, not accessed through local authorities. That needs to change. Because of an increasingly isolated suburban class, children growing up in Ireland by 2030 will have access to fewer services than children do today – despite the fact that there will be more of these children, and their parents will be richer than we are today. Community services, when properly resourced through local taxation, can foster community spirit, reduce social isolation, and find local solutions to local problems. Carbon and water rate taxes can be levied at different rates to encourage or discourage various behaviours, and to attract new households and businesses to particular areas. We need to allow authorities to actively compete for new businesses, new home-owners, and the best teachers and educational opportunities.

Transparent, properly accountable administrations, with differing competencies, could be built up over time: localities that can specialise in agriculture over commerce, say, or bio-technology, or green-tech start-ups, or organisations that offer services in large, high density urban areas. People can choose where to live and work, and the range of services offered by different local authorities (based on the types and rates of taxation they levy) would be a deciding factor in the decision of a business or household to locate in one county or another.

Leadership at local-government level is required in order to avoid short-term planning pressures, to discourage encroachment from the national executive, and to provide for education to broaden the public's understanding of higher urban densities and better-quality urban design. The fact that local government is not involved in health, education and policing reduces the stake that people feel they have in local government. Local authorities can change the way they do business to increase public participation in local initiatives.

Take Offaly, for example. Imagine that tomorrow, Offaly County Council decided to try to attract new information and communications technology start-ups to Birr. How would they do it? They would levy a tax on water rates in Birr on residential properties, and use the taxation revenue to fit out, say, five buildings with ultra-high-speed next-generation fibre-optic networks. These networks embed fibre-optic cabling into the ground to deliver transfer speeds hundreds of times greater than Ireland's current information and communications grid can supply.

The rollout of these networks nationally is not cost-effective at the moment, but a *local* initiative to build a next-generation network would attract funding, investment and jobs. Say that Birr decided to invest as a test case, and ran fibre-optics to four or five buildings which are currently empty. Each building will be partitioned for, say, five companies with ten employees each. That's fifty new jobs.

The county council would then announce a competition to get the office space and the fibre-optic infrastructure (and, say, a development grant) internationally. One catch is that the company must hire 10 percent of its staff locally, and agree to stay in the same location for a minimum of two years. Some companies will stay and succeed, creating more jobs as they do so, and others will surely fail. The ones that succeed are likely to stay on, because the infrastructure is better and cheaper than anywhere else. Other high-tech companies will be attracted to the area because of the presence of the first set of successful companies. It is not stretching credibility to think of a high-tech hub in Birr, County Offaly, producing the next Google. If you build it, they will come.

Sponsoring local activism

Funding local authorities properly through differentiated (and locally determined) taxation is only one aspect of the regeneration of our local economies. The taxes really just change the range and number of services the local authorities can offer; in many cases, that will be all to the good. The other aspect of the development of local authorities is community-building. Here, the authorities must be tasked with giving individuals and groups funding, support, and a mandate to look after their area, to regenerate it, or to protect it.

I live, as I've said, in a small village in County Limerick called Murroe. Murroe has a set of concerned citizens who, on a completely voluntary basis, spend some of their time making the main street look nice: planting flowers, cleaning up, painting the local monument, and so on. If a bottle is broken on the street, they clean it up. Their presence makes all our lives better, because my kids won't cut their knees on that broken bottle. The concerned citizens represent, in economists' terms, a 'public good' – they are like the street-lights from the example I gave above.

In some areas, concerned citizens just pop up, self-select-ing onto the local committees set up to do this kind of work, or in some cases to win competitions like Tidy Towns. In other areas, especially in the newer housing estates and large high-density residential areas outside Dublin city and its sur-rounding counties, this self-selection is not taking place. Ironically, the prototype for community involvement has come from the poorer areas of Ireland. I want to argue that local authorities need to be resourced in order to empower those who, for whatever reason, don't feel like they have a mandate to act in the community's best interest.

Imagine local 'wardens', let's call them, each one respon-sible for three or four streets in a single area. For a tiny stipend, say a few thousand euro a year, the wardens clean up the broken bottles, tend to the plants, and carry out surveys and data collection for the government, such as the census and household checks. In areas where there are sites of his-toric interest or tourist attractions, the wardens work to enhance these sites. When new people come to the area, the wardens are tasked with introducing them to the communi-ty. The wardens are resourced and mandated to do this work. National competitions like Tidy Towns showcase the best and most innovative wardens.

The outlay is tiny, and the manpower exists already – in the retired community, which will only grow larger because of the increased longevity and good health of our popula-tion. The social benefits are, potentially, enormous.

JUSTICE FOR ALL

1 October 2050

Bobby was beaten up in school today. He showed pictures of his new niece to the class, and was ridiculed for it. At break time, one of the bigger kids decided to push Bobby around, and Bobby tripped awkwardly and cut his head. Bobby's phone alerted the teachers, who called the police. The bully in question was reprimanded, his parents were informed, and he was sent for mandatory counselling. Bobby was also sent home. Bobby's mother Sarah spent the afternoon looking after him. A Garda called to check on Bobby, but the family don't want to press charges, although Jack is seething.

WHITHER OUR COURT SYSTEM? HOW WILL TECHNOLOGY CHANGE THE GARDAÍ?

Today, two thousand houses in the UK are under twenty-four-hour video surveillance. Every room is monitored, every action observed and recorded. The scheme is to be rolled out nationally in 2010. The origins of the idea are benign: record and observe behaviours in the home, which might lead to anti-social behaviours on the streets, and correct them. Say that some of the families are not reading to their children at night. It is thought that reading to your children can help with memory and with schoolwork later on. So, having observed the lack of reading, 'experts' tell the families to read to their kids.

There are many things, in my opinion, wrong with this approach to social control. The erosion of the kinds of privacy we enjoy today, which I highlighted in Chapter 3, may well be complete by 2050, and we might see measures like this introduced into our own homes and businesses in the name of public safety and security. The technology continually to observe a human being's actions exists already. You see it on TV all the time on reality shows. By 2050, forty years of development will have made this technology smaller, smarter, and more ubiquitous. The price of privacy will be quite high: essentially unplugging oneself from the grid for certain activities. Given that everyone else will be using these technologies, the choice is, essentially, the choice to be alone. Those who decide that the level of intrusion into their personal lives is too high might become what author Ray Kurzweil calls 'neo-Luddites'[7].

FIFTEEN MINUTES OF PRIVACY

In 1811, weavers in Nottingham began to sabotage the newly invented power looms, which they saw as destroying their livelihoods. Legend has it that a young man named Ned Ludd broke two of these machines by accident. Apparently Ned wasn't the sharpest tool in the drawer. From that moment on, whenever factory machinery broke in suspicious circumstances, the owners were told that 'Ned Ludd did it'. When the displaced workers formed an organisation to stop the spread of the new machines, they called themselves Luddites. The Luddites were eventually brutally repressed by the Tory government of the day. They were the first organised movement to oppose the mechanised technology of the Industrial Revolution, and today they remain a symbol of that resistance.

Many of those campaigning against the encroachment of technology on their lives can be thought of as 'neo-Luddites'. The neo-Luddite position is one that we will see as growing in influence, especially around the displacement of low-end, relatively unskilled jobs due to technology, and also as the reduction in personal privacy becomes a key political battleground. The virtually constant use of trackable electronic communication technologies places great power in the hands of the person or organisation doing the tracking. Personal data is widespread and unevenly distributed, and the distinction between public and private information is blurring due to blogs, Twitter, and many other social media platforms. The problem can be summed up well by quoting Phil Zimmerman, the inventor of the Pretty Good Privacy (PGP) algorithm, which is widely used to encrypt data and communications. Phil writes that 'in the future, we'll have fifteen minutes of privacy'.

Returning to the theme of justice, the judicial system revolves around the collection of different kinds of evidence, and arguments presented to explain the presence of that evidence. Judges and juries decide what weight to give the evidence that is presented, and a ruling is made accordingly.

Today, the Gardaí are empowered by new laws to monitor your phone if they suspect you of a serious crime – and have the required scanning technology to do so. In 2050, though the technology to monitor suspected lawbreakers will have advanced, the need and desire to break those laws will still exist. Criminals will adapt, learning to block scanning signals and conduct their business away from prying electronic eyes. The problem of crime will still be with us, and with increased inequality, perhaps ghettos will be formed, where criminality and socially damaging practices and ways of life persist. The justice system, in short, will still be needed, as those on both sides adapt to the changes in monitoring technology and the encroachment of the state into individual homes.

BABY MONITOR

1 November 2050

Emily wears a wristband, which tells Maeve's phone everything about her daughter's current state: Emily's temperature, her cries, how long it has been since she last fed or soiled herself. Maeve can access her own records as a baby, and knows that Emily has the same type of sleeping patterns that she once had. It makes Maeve smile.

Jack's bill from the security company which monitors their home has arrived on his phone. Jack is thinking of finding another provider. The local authority owns the scanners built into every new home, and companies can use the scanners to provide their services. The security company has just increased its monthly rates, citing the wage increases given recently to their Chinese and American subcontractors. Jack runs his hands through his hair and starts a search for a new security company which has prices at least 15 percent lower than his current provider. As the search runs, he tunes into Emily's lifefeed, which is broadcast to his phone via her wristband, and listens to her breathing. Jack smiles to himself.

FACTOID: Today, 30 percent of PCs, cellphones, TVs and other electronic devices share audio, TV shows, video, data, Internet, and other digital content. The convergence of all forms of media towards a single, mobile platform is inevitable.

FACTOID: The 'Internet of Things' is a network of objects like household appliances. The idea is simple, but the implementation of it is very complicated. If all cans, books, shoes or parts of cars are equipped with minuscule identifying devices, daily life has to undergo a transformation. Things like running out of stock, or wasted products, or losing your shoes, will no longer exist, as we will know exactly what is being consumed on the other side of the globe. You will be able to Google your shoes, and they will tell you where they are in your house. Common theft will be a thing of the past, as we will know where a product is at all times – unless a criminal can bypass the wireless technologies connecting the stolen objects to the Internet of Things.

12

THE POWER OF AN IMAGINED END

> The power of an imagined end, and it literally can only
> be imagined, lies in its ability to influence present
> choices.
>
> DANIEL TAYLOR[1]

I began this book with this quote from Daniel Taylor. The
story I've just written is just that: a story. The end I've imagined by 2050 has a lot of positive aspects, and quite a few
negative ones. We have the ability, by imagining this end and
many more like it, to allow it to change our present choices.

Ireland's strategic direction must be chosen by an interplay of popular consensus and strong leadership. Too often,
important decisions that have long-term consequences are
taken to pacify short-term regional or party-political interests. The political system is built around these types of
squabbles, but in addressing only these concerns, we miss
the bigger picture. I'd like us to sketch out that picture
together. In this book, I've given some rough lines for such a
discussion.

East or West? Ireland needs to choose one and stick to it.

We are too small to satisfy all markets. Concentrating on embedding ourselves within the world's most likely long-term economic success story will shape our future as a nation.

Married or divorced? Old or young? Irish society will fragment along lines which were never drawn before. The rights of the elderly will be asserted as they become a political and economic force. The education of our children will need to be reformulated along lines designed to bring out their creativity if they are to survive and thrive in a global talent pool.

Hot and crowded? Ireland will experience moderate but sustained climate change in the next forty years, and this will bring costs (like flooding) and benefits (like real summers). The range of agricultural products the country generates will alter to accommodate the climate changes. Do we change our agricultural products ahead of schedule, or after three or four seasons of ruined crops? How do we plan to balance a larger population with the demands of agriculture and industry?

A nuclear Ireland? Will we transition to a nuclear-powered economy in time?

Education and the youth boom? Can we change our educational system fast enough so that those born in 2009 and 2010 have the skills to take advantage of the US economy's labour demands in 2030? Can we manage to keep those growing up rootless in suburbs around the country, with poor access to services, from becoming disaffected?

Health and wealth? Ireland's health care system will crack under the weight of a larger, older population unless massive resources are diverted to layering community services and hospital services, as well as home care, for older (and, not coincidentally, richer and more politically significant) citizens. Inequality of income and wealth will mean that those who can access modern health care privately will live longer, better lives than those who stay in the public system. Is that the Ireland we want?

Local government? We can increase social cohesion and reduce the disaffection of a rootless cohort of Irish youth at a stroke, while reducing usage of scarce natural resources by empowering local authorities to charge different taxes for different resources, and task the authorities to maintain social cohesion through a series of 'warden' programmes and to foster business growth through competition between themselves.

What kind of better Ireland would *you* like?

This is the power of an imagined end.

Epilogue: Another Fine Day

1 December 2050

The weather today is fine, and everyone is off. The Murphys go for a walk, and invite Patrick along with them. He pushes the pram proudly. Jack chose the colour purple for the pram, which everyone hates but him. Still, they got it for free with the new car, so no one complains too loudly. Emily snores as she is pushed along. Everyone coos. Patrick didn't know babies could snore. Someone takes a picture. Sarah feels a little older. Jack is making serious efforts to get to know Patrick, and it turns out that Patrick has a head for figures. He might make a good businessman one day, Jack thinks. Patrick stays over sometimes. Jack isn't too chuffed about it, but he says nothing.

The hills above Dublin Bay are crowded with houses, as they have been for forty years, but a nature trail cuts through the residential areas. The family make for the nature trail. This public amenity was paid for through local taxes, and Jack is proud of Jim for spearheading the movement to get the nature trail reclassified and renovated by local workers for the use of residents. Jack is also pretty sure the presence of the amenity has bumped up the price of his house, but he doesn't say that to anyone. Jim is keeping up well, Jack thinks, and doesn't look out of breath at all.

Jack's new business model has taken off, and he is working all the hours God sends. Sarah barely sees him, but she knows it's not forever. This is the nature of start-ups, and a day off like this is rare. Maeve has finished her Leaving Certificate, and is waiting for her results. She has decided to study business, like her father. Bobby's friends show up, having homed in on Bobby with their phones. He wants them to call him 'Rob' from now on, because he's getting older, and Bobby is a kid's name, he says. Just about everyone is humouring 'Rob', for the moment. Only Maeve insists on calling him 'Uncle Bobby' when Emily is around. 'Rob' makes a show of being annoyed at this.

They reach the top of the hill, and look around for a little while. Clouds roll in, and the sky turns dark. It looks like rain. Sarah hugs Jack. He hugs her back, although he's pretty sure she'd hug any warm object right now.

'Perfect,' he says.

POSTSCRIPT: INVITATION TO A ROW

This book isn't an academic piece. Academic writing is hard. You have to write for balance, for rigour, and use a very specialised language. Writing this book was also hard, but it was way more fun than I expected it to be, because I didn't write this book in a balanced way.

I wrote it to start a row. I want to invite you to that row, right now. Do you agree with me that Ireland will be a more unequal place in 2050? Do you see our privacy going up in smoke? Do you think that half of the couples in Ireland will be divorced by the middle of the century? Do you see the continual erosion of the Catholic Church as a good or a bad thing? What do you think we should be doing to get ourselves ready for the future?

Think about it, and let me know what you think. Visit *www.irelandin2050.com* if you're in the mood to rant about these and any of the other issues I have raised in this book.

And thanks for reading.

NOTES

CHAPTER 1: WRITING A HISTORY OF IRELAND'S FUTURE (PP. 24–40)

1. Daniel Taylor, *The Healing Power of Stories*, Doubleday Press, 1996.
2. Patrick Geoghegan, 'The union passes' in *The Irish Act of Union*. St Martin's Press, 1999, p. 110.
3. A phrase I've borrowed intentionally from J. M. Keynes, *Economic Possibilities for Our Grandchildren*, Reprinted in *Revisiting Keynes*, Edited by Lorenzo Pecchi and Gustavo Piga, MIT Press, 2008.
4. See the recent studies by Amárach Research, Economic Recovery Index, July 2009, available at *http://www.amarach.com/143.htm.*
5. See Bernard Harcourt, *Against Prediction: Profiling, Policing, and Punishing in an Actuarial Age*, University of Chicago Press, 2006. Also, Damian Corless, 'Don't Ask the Experts', *Irish Independent*, Saturday, 8 August 2009.
6. See J.K. Galbraith's *The Great Crash of 1929*, Mariner Books, 1997, for details of how, why, and when Fisher made his famous gaffe.
7. See the Irish Pensions Board website and downloadable publications on women and their pensions for details, at *http://www.pensions-board.ie/.*

CHAPTER 2: IRELAND IN THE WORLD (PP. 41–57)

1. Sourced from the Database Direct service of the Central Statistics Office, *www.cso.ie.*
2. *The Economist*, 'The luck of the Irish', 14 October 2004.

3.   Brendan Keenan, 'Emigration spectre back to haunt after 20 years', *Irish Independent*, 24 June 2008.

4.   Morgan Kelly, 'On the Likely Extent of Falls in Irish House Prices,' *Quarterly Economic Commentary: Special Articles, Economic and Social Research Institute (ESRI)*, vol. 2007(2-Summer), pp. 42-54.

5.   Nassim Nicholas Taleb, *The Black Swan*, Random House, 2006.

6.   Joseph J. Lee, *Ireland 1912-1985, Politics and Society*, Cambridge University Press, 1989, p. 521.

7.   For example, the 2006 A. T. Kearney/Foreign Policy Globalization Index.

8.   Kevin O'Rourke and Jeffrey G. Williamson, *Globalisation and History: The Evolution of a 19th Century Atlantic Economy*, MIT Press, 2003, Chapter 2.

9.   Michael J. O'Sullivan, *Ireland and the Global Question*, Syracuse University Press, 2006.

10. For example, National Intelligence Council Report, 2009: Global Trends 2025: A Transformed World, available at *http://www.dni.gov/nic/NIC_2025_project.html*.

11. For example, Dimitry Orlov, *Reinventing Collapse: The Soviet Example and American Prospects*, New Society Publishers, 2008.

12. All figures on population density come from *www.wolframalpha.com*.

13. J. J. Lee, *Ireland 1912-1985: Politics and Society*, Cambridge University Press, 1989, p. 631.

CHAPTER 3: THE DIVORCE BOMB: OUR FAMILIES, OUR KIDS AND OUR CULTURE (PP. 58–81)

1.   See Bella DePaulo's brilliant *Singled Out: How Singles Are Stereotyped, Stigmatized, and Ignored, and Still Live Happily Ever After,* St Martin's Press, 2006.

2.   See the Iona Institute's series of reports on divorce and marriage in Ireland at *www.ionainstitute.ie*.

3.   Central Statistics Office, *Equality in Ireland Report*, 2007.

4.   Michael Kimmel, *The Gendered Society*, Oxford University Press, 2000.

5.   Growing up in Ireland: A National Longditudinal study of Children, available at *http://www.growingup.ie/index.php?id=5*.

6.   There are serious measurement issues with the notion of 'single' parents, as discussed in Tony Fahey and Catherine Anne Field's Report to the Department of Family and Social Affairs in 2008: 'Families in Ireland: An analysis of patterns and trends', Dublin Stationary office, 2008.

7. See Daniel Webster Hollis III, *The History of Ireland*, Greenwood Press, 2001, p. 178.

8. Richard Hoggart, *The Uses of Literacy*, Transaction Publishers, 1998, p. 151.

9. Thomas Malone is a pioneer in this area, co-directing MIT's initiative 'Inventing the Organizations of the 21st Century,' which resulted in a landmark book, *The Future of Work: How the New Order of Business Will Shape Your Organization, Your Management Style, and Your Life*, Harvard Business School Press, 2004.

10. Ken Robinson, with Lou Aronica, *The Element: How Finding your Passion Changes Everything*, Allen Lane Publishers, 2009, page xiii.

11. For example: Department of Education and Science, Looking at Irish at Junior Cycle: Teaching and Learning in Post-Primary Schools, 2009, or Department of Education and Science, Department of Education & Science Statement of Strategy 2005 - 2007, or Department of Education and Science, Ready for Tomorrow's World: The Competencies of Irish 15-year-olds in PISA 2006. All reports are available on the *www.education.ie*.

12. See John Palfrey and Urs Gasser, *Born Digital: Understanding the First Generation of Digital Natives*, Basic Books, 2008.

13. S. L. Holloway and G. Valentine, *Cyberkids: Children in the Information Age*, Routledge-Falmer, 2003, p. 21.

14. To use a phrase borrowed from Moses Abramowitz, 'The Tasks of Economic History', *The Journal of Economic History*, Vol. 46, No. 2, (June, 1986), pp. 385-406.

15. See Alan Prout, *The Future of Childhood*, Routledge Press, 2004.

16. National Economic and Social Forum, Child Literacy & Social Inclusion Plenary Session, June 2009.

17. In his 1964 *Understanding Media: The Extensions of Man*, MIT Press, 1994.

18. According to developmental psychologist at Tufts University, Maryanne Wolf, quoted in Nicholas Carr's 'Is Google Making us Stupid?' Another soon-to-be classic on this problem is Chris Hedges *The Empire of Illusion: The End of Literacy and the Triumph of Spectacle*, Nation Books, 2009.

19. Nicholas Carr, 'Is Google Making Us Stupid?' *The Atlantic*, July/August, 2008.

20. See Bridget Murray, 'Data smog: newest culprit in brain drain', *APA Online*, Vol 29, No. 3, 1998, available at *http://www.apa.org/monitor/mar98/smog.html.*

21. For example, S. L. Holloway and G. Valentine, *Cyberkids: Children in The Information Age*, Routledge-Falmer Press, 2003, p. 231.

22. As reported in Brian Appleyards' 'Distraction', available at
     http://www.bryanappleyard.com/article.php?article_id=142 and also
     published in the *Sunday Times*, 20 July 2008.

CHAPTER 4: LEISURE SUIT LARRIES (PP. 82–90)

1. See Angus Maddison, *Contours of the World Economy, 1-2030AD:
    Essays in Macro-Economic History*, Oxford University Press, 2007,
    p. 307.
2. See Richard Watson, *Future Files: The 5 Trends That Will Shape the
    Next 50 Years*, Nicholas Brealey Publishing, 2008, page 222.
3. So the family of Oscar Weber Bilby claim in Josh Ozersky, *The
    Hamburger: A History*, Yale University Press, 2008.
4. Ibid.
5. See http://www.edge.org/3rd_culture/shirky08/shirky08_index.html
    for details of Shirky's talk.
6. Barry Schwartz, *The Paradox of Choice*, Harper Perennial, 2004.

CHAPTER 5: THE ENVIRONMENT OF IRELAND IN 2050:
HOT, FLAT AND CROWDED (PP. 91–109)

1. See *http://esa.un.org/unpp/* for the details.
2. Source: Population Division of the Department of Economic and
    Social Affairs of the United Nations Secretariat, World Population
    Prospects: The 2006 Revision and World Urbanization Prospects:
    The 2005 Revision, *http://esa.un.org/unpp*.
3. For details, see *http://epp.eurostat.ec.europa.eu/pls/portal/docs/PAGE/
    PGP_PRD_CAT_PREREL/PGE_CAT_PREREL_YEAR_2005/PGE_CAT_PRER-
    EL_YEAR_2005_MONTH_04/3-08042005-EN-AP.PDF.*
4. See *http://geography.nuim.ie/ICARUS/* for details.
5. See *www.ipcc.org* for details of this model.
6. For example the Environmental Protection agency:
    http://www.epa.ie/whatwedo/climate/climatechangeresearch/ and the
    Department of the Environment, Heritage, and Local Government:
    http://www.environ.ie/en/ and their White Paper: Delivering a
    Sustainable Energy Future for Ireland.
7. Trinity College Dublin's Centre for the Environment *http://www.nat-
    uralscience.tcd.ie/CENV2006/index.php* and NUI Galway's
    Environmental Change Institute
    http://www.nuigalway.ie/eci/research/climate_change.html are also at the
    forefront of research in this area.
8. *http://geography.nuim.ie/ICARUS/test/exec/scenarios.pdf.*
9. Paul Cunningham, *Ireland's Burning*, Poolbeg Press, 2008.
10. So there is a possibility of an Irish viniculture by 2050!

11. See 'July rainfall in Cork heaviest since 1975' for details.

12. A masterly account of the impact of the highly improbable is Nassim Nicholas Taleb, *The Black Swan*, Random House, 2007.

13. Again, Taleb's *The Black Swan* and his 2004 *Fooled by Randomness* (Random House) give clues on how to 'robustify' ourselves against low probability, high impact events.

14. The 2008 Forfas report into water usage and planning writes that most local authorities will be fine regarding water shortages up to 2013 at forecasted levels of demand, but 'without further investment in water treatment capacity, Athlone, Dublin, and Galway are forecast to also experience deficits [in water] by 2013.'

15. See Gerard Mills article on the subject in *Irish Geography*, 33:2, pp. 99-116, 2000 for more on this definition.

16. See Forfas report, 2008, pg 6.

17. See Annika Carlsson-Kanyama and Mireille Faist, 'Energy Use in the Food Sector: A data survey', 2000, available at *http://www.infra.kth.se/fms/pdf/energyuse.pdf*.

CHAPTER 6: POWERING A POST-INDUSTRIAL IRELAND (PP. 110–119)

1. Julian Simon, *The Ultimate Resource*, Princeton University Press, 1996, p. 162.

2. Dimitry Orlov, *Reinventing Collapse: The Soviet Example and American Prospects*, New Society Publishers, 2008.

3. Stephen Mulvey, 'Wildlife defies radiation', BBC News, 20 April 2006. Available at *http://news.bbc.co.uk/2/hi/europe/4923342.stm*.

CHAPTER 7: PEOPLE, PRODUCTION AND THE NATURE OF WORK (PP. 120–145)

1. Thomas Hager, *The Alchemy of Air*, Harmony Books, 2008.

2. Hamish McRae, *The World in 2020: Power, Culture, and Prosperity*, Havard Business School Press, 1994, Chapter 4.

3. Edward Nell, *The General Theory of Transformational Growth: Keynes after Sraffa*, Cambridge University Press, 1998, pp. 18-30.

4. Ibid, p. 102 especially.

CHAPTER 8: INCUBATORS OF APATHY, DISCONNECTION AND DELIRIUM? OUR ROADS, OUR CITIES AND OUR SUBURBS (PP. 146–157)

1. See Michael Daly, Liam Delaney, Colm Harmon, Peter Doran and Malcolm MacLachlan, 2009, 'Naturalistic monitoring of the affect-heart rate relationship: A Day Reconstruction Study,' Working Papers 2009/01, Geary Institute, University College Dublin.

2. Tim Lomax and David Schrank, '2009 Urban Mobility Report', Texas Transportation Institute report number 130001-06242009-DS, available at http://mobility.tamu.edu/ums/.

3. Jared Diamond's influential study 'Guns, Germs, and Steel', W.W. Norton, 1999 provides background on our previous social architectures.

4. See Edward J. Nell, *The General Theory of Transformational Growth*, Cambridge University Press, 1998, Chapter 3 for more details on the effects of changes in the urban/rural divide.

5. There are many reasons for this outward movement, among them the price of land, planning regulations, the circumvention of these regulations by special interests, and our historically low population density. See Frank McDonald and James Nix, *Chaos at the Crossroads*, Gandon Editions, 2005.

6. See *The Economist*, 21 June 2008, 'The Big Sort'.

7. Michael Peillon, Mary Corcoran, and Jane Gray, 'Civic Engagement and the Governance of Irish Suburbs', The Policy Institute, Trinity College, Dublin, 2006.

CHAPTER 9: HEALTH (PP. 158–175)

1. The world's oldest woman, Edna Parker, died in 2008 at 115 years old

2. Richard Watson, *Future Files: The 5 Trends That Will Shape the Next 50 Years*, Nicholas Brealey Publishing, 2008.

3. James Canton, *The Extreme Future*, Plume Publishers, 2007.

4. Richard Watson, Future Files: The 5 Trends That Will Shape the Next 50 Years, Nicholas Brealey Publishing, 2008.

5. Recently the Society of Actuaries in Ireland has called for this measure: See. *www.actuaries.ie/Press%20Office/Press%20Releases/080528%20Green%20Paper%20press%20release.pdf*

6. Tim Callan, Arthur Van Soest and John R. Walsh, Tax Structure and Female Labour Market Participation: Evidence from Ireland IZA, Discussion Paper No. 3090, 2007, *http://papers.ssrn.com/sol3/papers.cfm?abstract_id=1027897*.

7. Lisa Lzabo, 'Number of Americans Taking Antidepressants doubles', *USA Today*, 3 August 2009.

8. E. Larson, Community Factors in the Development of Antibiotic Resistance. [Electronic Version]. Annual Review of Public Health 28, 2007, pp. 437-447.

9. 'Cell Movements and the Shaping of the Vertebrate Body' in Chapter 21 of *Molecular Biology of the Cell*, 4th edition, edited by Bruce Alberts, Garland Science, 2002.

10. Ruth Barrington, 'Health, medicine and politics in Ireland, 1900-70', Dublin Institute of Public Administration, 2000.

CHAPTER 10: INEQUALITY AND EXCLUSION: HOMELESS IN DUBLIN IN 2050? (PP. 176–188)

1. Charles McCarthy, 'The decade of upheaval: Irish trade unions in the nineteen sixties', Dublin Institute of Public Administration, 1973, pp. 219-220.
2. Focus Ireland's yearly reports make for interesting, and harrowing, reading on this point. See *http://www.focusireland.ie/html/education/causes.htm* for details.
3. Flavio Cunha & James J. Heckman, 2009. 'The Economics and Psychology of Inequality and Human Development,' NBER Working Papers 14695, National Bureau of Economic Research.
4. Richard Wilkinson and Kate Pickett, *The Spirit Level: Why More Equal Societies Almost Always Do Better*, Allen Lane Press, 2009.
5. Ibid.
6. Here I paraphrase *www.turbulenceahead.com*'s Gerard O'Neill, Director of Amárach Research, Dublin.
7. Here the Conference of Religious in Ireland (*www.cori.ie*) and the Central Statistics Office provide very different definitions of poverty. I prefer the CORI definition.
8. See Amartya Sen, Geoffrey Hawthorn and John Muellbauer *The Standard of Living*, Cambridge University Press, 1987, p. 18.
9. Ibid, p. 18.
10. CORI Justice, Statistical Yearbook of Ireland, Chapter 3.
11. According to Makeroom, the homelessness research and advocacy group, see *www.makeroom.ie*.
12. Joe Saxton and Elisha Evans, 'The Future of Homelessness?' Briefing paper on the Future of Homelessness as part of the London Housing Foundation's IMPACT programme, available at *http://www.thinkcs.org/downloads/The_Future_of_Homelessness.pdf*

CHAPTER 11: OUR GOVERNMENT: NATIONAL, REGIONAL AND LOCAL (PP. 189–205)

1. See Bruce Sterling, *Tomorrow Now*, Random House, 2003, p. 160, and Chris Hedges, *Empire of Illusion: The And of Literacy and the Triumph of Spectacle*, Nation Books, 2009, Chapter 3, and Neil Postman and Andrew Postman, *Amusing Ourselves to Death: Public Discourse in the Age of Show Business*, Penguin, 2005.
2. C. Wright Mills, *The Politics of Truth: Selected writings of C. Wright Mills*, edited by John H. Summers, Oxford University Press, 2008.

3. For examples, see Sarah Burke, *Irish Apartheid*, New Island Press, 2009.

4. Mark Callanan and Justin F. Keogan, 'Local Government in Ireland', Institute of Public Administration, 2003, Chapters 2 and 3 especially.

5. Mark Callanan and Justin F. Keogan, 'Local Government in Ireland, Institute of Public Administration', 2003, p. 21-23.

6. See R. Kenneth Carty, *Party and Parish Pump*, Wilfrid Laurier University Press, 1981, for details of the 1977 rate removal and an excoriating analysis of party politics during the run up to the 1977 budget and the fallout afterwards.

7. Ray Kurzweil, *The Age of Spiritual Machines*, Phoenix Press, 1999, page 228.

CHAPTER 12: THE POWER OF AN IMAGINED END (PP. 206–208)

1. Daniel Taylor, *The Healing Power of Stories*, Doubleday, 1996.